the 7 secrets
of the
Silver Shoes
Principles for Success On and Off the Field

the 7 secrets *of the* Silver Shoes

Principles for Success On and Off the Field

foreword by
BARRY SWITZER

by NFL and Sooner Legend
JOE WASHINGTON

TATE PUBLISHING
AND ENTERPRISES, LLC

The Seven Secrets of the Silver Shoes
Copyright © 2015 by Joe Washington. All rights reserved.

No part of this publication may be reproduced, stored in a retrieval system or transmitted in any way by any means, electronic, mechanical, photocopy, recording or otherwise without the prior permission of the author except as provided by USA copyright law.

The opinions expressed by the author are not necessarily those of Tate Publishing, LLC.

Published by Tate Publishing & Enterprises, LLC
127 E. Trade Center Terrace | Mustang, Oklahoma 73064 USA
1.888.361.9473 | www.tatepublishing.com

Tate Publishing is committed to excellence in the publishing industry. The company reflects the philosophy established by the founders, based on Psalm 68:11,
"The Lord gave the word and great was the company of those who published it."

Book design copyright © 2015 by Tate Publishing, LLC. All rights reserved.
Cover design by Christina Hicks
Interior design by Mary Jean Archival

Published in the United States of America
ISBN: 978-1-61777-303-7
1. Biography & Autobiography / Sports
2. Self-Help / Personal Growth / Success
14.12.16

FOREWORD

By
Barry Switzer

I own some of life's greatest titles: son, brother, husband, father, and grandfather. But I have to admit the title of "coach" resonates deep and conjures up many visions and memories. But mostly, I see the faces of young men I have had the honor to coach. My book, *Bootlegger's Boy*, was published following the end of my coaching career at the University of Oklahoma and I had no way of knowing that in a matter of months after leaving the Sooners I'd be entering the professional football coaching ranks as the Head Coach of "America's Team" – the Dallas Cowboys.

Counting the days as coach at Arkansas before Oklahoma, I have coached over a thousand players. And I have coached some great ones. Which brings us to mention one player in particular: Joe Dan Washington, Jr., or as he will ever be to me and thousands of fans, "Little Joe". His father/coach, Joe, Sr., was "Big Joe", and he taught Little Joe how to play the game like it's supposed to be played.

When Little Joe arrived on campus of the University of Oklahoma back in 1972, our expectations were high. Soakin' wet he may have weighed 160 pounds. But from the moment he ran the ball in practice we knew he would be special. I had never seen and still haven't seen anyone who could bring an entire crowd to it's feet while they suck in all the air in the stadium, leaving fans awe-struck time and time again. Even while gaining just a handful of yards his runs were absolutely spectacular. I mean every time he touched the ball, we expected it to be "showtime." He found seams to run that no one else saw, darted away from towering linemen and stutter-stepped his way down the field, but it was his ability to hurdle and leap over opponents that made us all hold our breath.

And, yes, he wore silver shoes, painting them himself just before the game with Kansas State when he was a freshman. One coach made some comment about the Sooners being undisciplined because we "even let some guy wear a different color of shoes." Damn right we did. And when we played his team later, Little Joe came to me and said, "Coach, what should I do?" I said, "Go out there and put 200 yards on their ass!" He had 198 by halftime. Current OU Head Coach, Bob Stoops talks about painting his football shoes silver when he was a teenager "just like Joe Washington."

Year after year, Little Joe made every All-American team including the UPI, AP, Walter Camp Foundation, The Sporting News, and the NEA list. He came in 3rd for the

Heisman Trophy behind Archie Griffin from Ohio State and USC's Anthony Davis. He finished up his college career with 4,071 rushing yards, 39 Touchdowns to his credit and 19 plus games of 100 yards. Incredible, especially because Joe only played half of every game; we were usually that far ahead by half-time. He was a huge factor in the Sooners claim to two back-to-back National Championships in '74 and '75. Little Joe was a first round draft pick (#4) in 1976, and went on to have a stellar career in the NFL, eventually winning a Super Bowl with the Washington Redskins in 1982.

You'd think with all these honors and notoriety he would be a little arrogant, or somewhat self assured – well, you don't know Little Joe. He is one of the most humble, unassuming guys you'll ever meet. Don't get me wrong – he loves to laugh, but mostly at himself. You know, I never saw him celebrate on the field after a stunning run or a score. He'd toss the ball to a teammate or the ref and just act like it was business as usual. He still owns a quiet confidence and to this day looks like he could suit up and dazzle us all over again.

I love Little Joe and I'm so glad I get to see him often around the campus and in our home. He is just family to us. Heck, he was our kids' favorite babysitter. He still calls me "Coach" and credits me with seeing his potential and helping him become a man, etc. Hell, Joe – I know the truth. As a player you were a gift any coach begs God for – and you made me look better than I was. Sure, there were players who made me strive to be a better coach, but you, Little Joe, inspired me to be a better man. Thank you for our effortless, timeless friendship. *The*

Seven Secrets of the Silver Shoes should be required reading – it will give others an opportunity to see what I've known for more than forty years. Yours is an enduring legacy and a blue print on how to win at the game of life.

—Barry Switzer
Norman, Oklahoma

"Like smoke through a keyhole."

—Comment by Darrell Royal, Head Coach and later Athletic Director for the University of Texas, on the running ability of Joe Washington

"In an era of prolific success and high-profile personalities, perhaps no player was more emblematic of Barry Switzer's brilliant run than Joe Washington. Joe's electrifying ability helped the Sooners capture three straight Big 8 titles and two national championships. Interestingly, through the years his star continues to glimmer like his famed silver shoes. He is a legendary figure whose accomplishments stretch across many generations. His enduring popularity is a testament to his career, the kindness he continually shows people and the great Oklahoma tradition."

~ Joe Castiglione, Athletic Director for The University of Oklahoma

"Joe Washington and his silver shoes remain colorful links to Coach Switzer's back-to-back national Championships in 1974-75. I appreciate Joe's friendship, his ongoing support of Oklahoma athletics and unwavering passion for the Sooners."

~ Bob Stoops, Head Football Coach, University of Oklahoma

DEDICATION

Pertrilla (Pat) Denita Washington Herbert
September 16, 1954 – September 5, 2014

I am dedicating this book to my truest and greatest fan ever—my sister, Pat. There aren't any words to describe what Pat means (meant) to me and my brother, Kim. Maybe the word "everything" will do. Pat's presence allowed us to connect with Mom. Hopefully, between her and mom, they can put in a good word for me up there. I miss her terribly.

INTRODUCTION

When writing this book, I quickly discovered that for me to describe my experiences and memories with enough clarity and accuracy that it made them true to life, I had to really examine and scrutinize every detail in a manner I had never done before. Plus, you really see things differently when you get to be a certain age. In doing so, I discovered the depth of love and degree of meaning to the word family that I had never seen before: a dad, who believed that hard work was a cure-all, a sister who was so loyal that it would make Judas cringe, a younger brother who was more of a big brother to me than I was to him, and a mom…a mom who was so many things to me that it is difficult to put them all down. She was loving, nurturing, exemplary, smart, God-loving, athletic, loyal, stern, supportive, and cool–just plain cool; cool enough to wear a baseball cap backwards and sit on the blacktop and shoot marbles with her kids. She and Dad both accommodated us in every way possible. If it was something we wanted to do, they provided us with the tools to help us learn, improve, or master any skill.

I grew up with parents that shielded me and my siblings from ever really being affected by the Jim Crow laws; we didn't know we weren't allowed to enter through the front of some restaurants; we simply thought going to the back meant getting the freshest and hottest food; even extra food straight from the chef. In a lot of cases, this was literally true because usually my dad had one of his players working at the café helping to cook. I was taught that I was equal to any other person on this earth, which later enabled me to easily fit in when we attended a "white" school.

Viewing my life as a spectator in the audience, I saw the circumstances that determined many of the decisions I made and paths that I took; the individuals who impacted those decisions, and the events of the world that changed its landscape forever. I realized that the two different environments in which I was raised, as different as they were, and were supposed to be, really were not that different after all…segregated/desegregated.

My dad was the athletic director, head football coach and head track coach at Hilliard High School in Bay City, Texas. In the 60's, Bay City began the process of desegregation which would ultimately close Hilliard High School and cause my dad to lose his position as head coach. Unwilling to accept anything less than a head coaching job, he found a comparable position in Port Arthur, Texas at Port Arthur Lincoln High School. Though they, too, were working toward desegregation, Lincoln High School would remain open and Dad could remain head coach throughout the desegregation movement. This also meant he would be the head coach of the high school football team on which my brother and I would play.

Since I was too small to master the regulation height hurdle with the correct form, my dad built my first hurdle and customized it to my size, in order to teach me the art of hurdling. The art of hurdling would later turn out to be one of the greatest gifts he ever gave me.

My mother showed me the power of accepting others, of having confidence in my unique talents and abilities, and the value of never taking those gifts for granted. I learned from teachers and every coach I had. The individuals who influenced me so greatly were the ones who taught me the principles discussed in this book. I didn't always adhere to them perfectly myself, or follow them, or even acknowledge them, but the principles were there and I knew what they were. These life principles will guide you whether you are a teacher, athlete, salesman, or parent. They work, not because I say so, but because they are fundamental to character building. You may have forgotten the principles, but you know them, even depend on them. Perhaps you once believed in them and will believe in them again. Eventually, we all come back to them.

I will be remembered for the silver shoes, but it was never about the shoes. It was *who* was in the shoes, who *put* me in the shoes, who *kept* me in the shoes, who *believed* in me in the shoes, and who shaped my character to *fit* the shoes. It is for each of them I share these "secrets" and offer my heartfelt gratitude to them all.

This is my desire for each one who reads this book. The thought that someone's life could be changed for the better because of the principles which have guided my life, drove me to write the book. If the life of a single person can be improved or inspired to pursue their own dreams through this book, that means more to me than my National Championship or Super Bowl rings.

—Joe Washington

SECRET #1

The Silver Shoes Come to Life

"I always knew it wasn't about the shoes"

For those who may not know, I became known as the running back who wore the "silver shoes." The shoes became my icon throughout the balance of my career, but the story behind how they evolved has a much bigger meaning.

From the time my little brother and I could walk, we hung around our dad, Joe Washington, Sr., who, as previously stated, was a high school football coach. When I say "coach," I mean "coach." Back in that day, the coach was father, mother, confidant, disciplinarian, bus driver, and trainer. Most of all, he had to have skin as tough as nails.

Football was in our blood. We loved the atmosphere, the dreams associated with the game, you name it, but, that is another story. Even as youngsters, we did whatever we could to help, (we thought we were helping, but, we were mostly in the way), so we could be around our dad and football. We would carry water, haul tackling dummies, run errands, carry towels to players when they needed to wipe their faces, and perform a million other jobs, including being in charge of the equipment. Our help in that regard, for the most part, consisted of being the first ones to open the boxes when new stuff came in for the team. We were first to see the new helmets, shoulder pads, jerseys, pants, but we were most excited about the shoes.

Until the 1960's, a football player, or aspiring player, had only one color choice in footwear – black. As youngsters, my brother and I saw how Lenny Moore, the NFL Hall of Fame halfback, "spatted" his shoes with white tape to make them look different than the normal old black shoe. Then, some players started putting a strip of white tape around the instep of their black shoes. During that time, *Riddell*, (the *Nike* of that time), introduced the XP shoe model featuring a white instep support strap and white ankle support strap. The first two players I recall that wore white shoes were Fred "the Hammer" Williams and Joe Namath. During that period, we noticed the difference between the all black shoes and the ones taped around the instep, and the shoes that were just white. Initially, my brother and I didn't have much choice about the shoes we managed to get our hands on. They were usually leftovers after the team received their shoes and usually three to six sizes too large, but at this point…we had seen the light.

My brother and I loved all sports and were good at all of them, but our love for football went to another level. As stated, we had watched from the sidelines for years as Dad coached and we could hardly wait for the day when we both would play together for our dad. We finally got to play for

Dad when I was a senior and Kim was in his sophomore year. At the time, we were totally convinced, without a doubt, white shoes were the way to go.

I did go through a progression of wearing different brands of black shoes before wearing white, then silver shoes. I wore the basic black shoes during high school except for my senior year when Kim convinced Dad to allow us to wear white shoes for Homecoming. We just believed the white shoes looked faster and sleeker on your feet. And boy, did they look good with our purple and gold uniforms! Oh, yeah, we had the gold shoe strings goin' on, too. I have them to this day, but they have a coat of silver paint on them.

Again, football was something I loved at a level I cannot describe. I would play anywhere, anytime, with anyone. While at Lincoln High School in Port Arthur, I began to think about where I wanted to go to college. Initially, I thought about where my favorite pro players had attended: Joe Bellino and Roger Staubach – Naval Academy; O.J. Simpson and Mike Garrett – USC; Pete Maravich and Billy Cannon – LSU (I really related to Pete, a basketball player who also played for his dad and could do jaw-dropping things with the ball); Gale Sayers – Kansas; Chris Gilbert and Jim Bertelsen – Texas; Warren McVea–Houston; Floyd Little and Ernie Davis – Syracuse; Archie Manning–Old Miss.

I was honored to have been recruited by just about every big college program in the nation, but I will say during this time, on a side note, I noticed out of all the major universities, Oklahoma was the only university whose football team wore white shoes – coaches and staff included. I didn't think this was a big deal at the time, so I just filed it away in my mind. As I got serious about choosing a school, every detail came to light and I was asking relative questions: Could I get into dental school? How far was the dorm from classes? Did the school provide tutors? Would I be able to keep my football number? Yes, I even considered each school's team uniforms, and man, those white shoes Oklahoma wore sure looked cool on everybody!

The story is true that President Lyndon Johnson called personally to invite me and family to his LBJ Ranch at the request of Texas coach, Darrell Royal to try and sway me away from OU. This was after Johnson was out of office. I suppose we could have gone just out of courtesy, but Mom felt it would have been misleading to make the visit because she knew my mind was pretty well made up, so we didn't go. An ESPN article by Ivan Maisel titled, "Joe Washington's Presidential Courting" gives a few more details.

In the end, the University of Oklahoma won out and University of Oklahoma football legend, Greg Pruitt, had a great deal to do with my choice to become a Sooner. Plus, I wanted to be a part of the long line of OU greats like Billy Vessels, Clendon Thomas, Steve Owens, and Jakie Sandefer.

Greg Pruitt was from Houston, Texas, seventy miles from Bay City where my family lived until 1964. He was also coached by Wendell Mosley, who would later become a coach at OU, a connection very important to me through the years. Greg was an All-American, a Heisman Trophy finalist and I loved his approach to the game; always encouraging and positive. He was a senior at OU when I entered as a freshmen and the opportunity for me to play with Greg was exciting. Foremost, was the fact we were close in size so I could immediately relate. I was definitely on a mission to play in the same backfield with the great Greg Pruitt.

Playing for the University of Oklahoma was a puzzle with all the right pieces fitting into the right places. Being a part of a team like Oklahoma was a dream come true and when I arrived in Norman, Oklahoma for my visit to the campus I found the athletic dorm – it was named "Washington House." Right then, I knew it was meant to be!

Though it took me and my little brother, Kenneth, whom we called Kim, a few years to understand that we "had a thing" with shoes, it took me nearly thirty years to realize what a cool gift was given to me when my brother suggested painting my shoes silver. And, though specific to me, the story behind how the silver shoes came to be is one that reflects the importance of people in my life.

The beginning...

Once I made my college choice and knew I was heading to Oklahoma to play for the Sooners, little did I know that I would only wear white shoes for warms ups and an occasional practice. My white shoes from home never made the trip to Oklahoma because my brother had already figured I wouldn't be wearing them. As mentioned earlier, the entire OU team, including coaches and staff wore white shoes so one day in July, without any hesitation in his voice, Kim suggested a change, "You should paint your shoes silver…silver with red shoestrings. They all wear white – you got to be different!"

We didn't talk about the fact I would be a freshman playing on one of the most storied programs in college football or how it would be received by other players including the All-Americans on the team. We may not have talked about it, but it was on my mind. After Kim kept going on and on about how good they were going to look, we decided to come up with a prototype, so the next day I went out and bought a can of silver spray paint, red paint with a small brush for the trim, and red shoe strings. Well, as you can imagine, the shoes were breathtaking, things of beauty. We were speechless. The shoes were spectacular and they sparkled. I was so excited I couldn't wait to get to Norman and wear those shoes.

I didn't paint my game shoes they gave us to wear for the first four games despite my younger brother pushing and asking, "When are you doing it? When are you doing it?"

I first painted the shoes on a game day just before we were to play the University of Colorado. My brother and I talked on the phone earlier in the week and he asked about the shoes and when I was planning to wear them. I told him I would wear the shoes for the upcoming game against Colorado. So, after pregame warm ups and just before going back out to play the game, I went to one of the bathroom stalls in the locker room with the can of silver paint Kim and I had bought before I had to report to football camp. I began to spray those babies silver until they glistened like brand new quarters.

I didn't realize that Dan Ruster, a senior, was in the stall next to me. He got up from the 'john', looked over the top of the stall and asked, "Lil Joe, what the hell are you doing?"

I told him and Dan said, "Well, why are you doing it now – why didn't you do it earlier?"

I told him if I had painted them earlier the coaches could easily tell me to change shoes, but because we were on our way out to play, there wouldn't be time to make me change, nor would they be paying attention to my shoes.

I could hear the Equipment Manager, Jack Baer complaining about the smell of the paint as it permeated the locker room area. We lost that game, our only loss that season – probably because we were all high!

No one other than Dan Ruster said anything about my silver shoes, none of the coaches made remarks; nothing. I talked to my brother, later in the week and he asked how it went. I told him it went great because no one mentioned anything about the shoes. I hadn't painted the stripes red yet, nor, had I added the red shoe strings, so the shoes may have looked somewhat white.

The next game was a home game. It would be the first game I was to start playing in the same backfield as the sensational, Greg Pruitt. I sprayed the shoes again, but this time on a Thursday. I then added the red stripes along with the red shoestrings. I took a deep breath and just sat there looking at them because now there was no turning back – I had done it. I had just painted my team-issued game shoes silver and red. During pregame warm-ups I went through my usual routine wearing heavier shoes, not my actual game shoes. We went back into the locker room for the final time then I waited until everyone went out onto the field. I pulled the painted shoes out of a special bag I kept in the bottom of my locker under some other shirts and stuff, slipped into my version of a "phone booth" (actually, a bathroom stall), and put on the silver shoes, ran out, took the field and again had a super game. Still no one said anything about the shoes, not even Dan Ruster this time. That was about to change.

It was customary to view film with the offensive team every Sunday following a Saturday game. Coach Switzer was the Offensive Coordinator at the time and he presided over the meeting and ran the film. We were studying the film, business as usual, while Coach was making comments about our performance. There was nothing out of the ordinary until he got to one play where I carried the ball and it was actually a good run. He ran the clip again. During those days the film was 16mm and the projectors had reverse buttons you clicked to rewind the film. He complimented me on the run, and then, I heard the click, then another click and another. He still didn't say anything. By this time I am totally shaking. Then, Coach clicks off the projector and says, "Little Joe, what are those things on your feet?"

I replied, "My silver shoes, Coach," but, it seemed as if it took forever for me to get those words out.

He responded with a simple, "Okay," and never said another word about them. Coach Switzer's silence spoke volumes about the shoes, about me, about him, and our relationship when he became Head Coach the next year, but that, too, is another story. Coach's reaction was his way of giving me permission to wear the silver shoes.

Thus, the silver shoes were born and became a part of who I was and how I was recognized by fans across America. Over the years people remember me as "the guy who wore the silver shoes who played for Oklahoma."

In retrospect, I see that what Kim and I were really striving for must have been a desire for uniqueness, otherwise the white shoes Oklahoma wore would have been okay. To this day, I can't believe that all Coach said was, "Okay." What amazes me more is the fact he convinced then Head Coach, Chuck Fairbanks, it was okay. I thought then that it was a test to really see what kind of kid I was or maybe how the rest of the team would react. I even thought, *Gee, what the hell would Gregg Pruitt think?* Well, either way, I became totally committed to Barry Switzer, the man whom I call, "my coach" to this day.

Looking back now I see what a special gift my brother gave me. Sure, all my hard work, blood, sweat and tears are what made my silver shoes dance. But, maybe it was my brother's good karma that gave them "wings." After all, at his age, how many of us would give to a sibling something that we ourselves could use? Until writing this book, I am not sure I ever even recognized his generosity and unselfishness. Kim was proud of me and instead of keeping the silver shoe idea for himself, he wanted me to run with it. So, the secret behind the "silver shoes" probably wasn't what most people thought. Without the influence of my brother, I would never have had the iconic symbol for which I am most known and the thing that made me a bit more unique.

Recognizing how we, as individuals, are impacted by others is key to understanding ourselves and who we are. Two scenarios that will quickly sum this up are as follows:

Scenario One: You are the only human being on Earth. You have never interacted with another human, nor will you.

Scenario Two: You have been loved and nurtured from birth. Your parents are both well educated professionals and they closely monitor your interactions within society to see that you only have positive influences.

Obviously, both of these scenarios are to the extreme, but it is easy to see that the first scenario would produce a shell of a human with little personality and lesser coping skills than the one in the second scenario.

It isn't just our family members that impact us, though they generally have the greatest degree of impact. We are all influenced, good or bad, by our friends, co-workers, fictitious characters in movies and books, athletes, even criminals and wrongdoers – they all provide us with characteristic barometers by which we gauge ourselves. Our personalities are developed either through emulation or rejection.

The importance of others in our lives must not be discounted, just as the importance of how our actions might possibly be impacting others. Be aware of your surrounding influences and allow yourself to credit others for impacting you. Whether you consciously or subconsciously chose to imitate certain traits in others; whether you admire or abhor them, you cannot say they don't have an impact upon you – be it positive and something you will attach to yourself, or something negative you determine never to allow yourself to be. Often, experiences with others provide us with the ability to be more understanding, because, if we were in another's shoes, our responsibility level would be different as well as our perspective and approach toward life. Even then, there is still something that impacts you.

During my career, I would notice kids, and even adults wearing painted silver shoes. It was a kick to see others emulate a tradition that had a special meaning for me. Since my football days preceded the big athletic shoe companies who now name shoes for various athletes, there was never a "Joe Washington Silver" offered. That would have been really cool! But, encouraging people, kids and adults to be unique, to "paint their own shoes" if you will, really was a big deal to me.

But, I always knew it was not about the shoes. I really believe the seven "secrets" I want to share with you in this book were the real reasons for my success. Success is not always something that puts you in a record book or in the cash deposit line at the bank. Success is about owning a passion for what you do and the means to find your own passion.

The silver shoes did not make me faster. Hard work did. The silver shoes did not make me a better team player. Attitude did. The silver shoes did not make my touchdowns worth more than six points. (Well, maybe they *did* look a little better in silver.) The shoes were a symbol to me of something that was inside of Joe Washington that had been placed there by a loving family, great coaches, and the many people upon whose shoulders I have been allowed to stand.

SECRET #2

Sometimes You Have to Go Backward Before You Can Go Forward

It has never entered my mind to give up on something. I have always thought of myself as an optimist with the conscience of a realist. I am always of the outlook that there has to be a way to get it done: buying time, or getting help and getting it done some how; in some way. Sometimes all it takes is a step backward to see the whole picture and gain a new perspective in order to make a decision. I live by a simple creed; if you hold onto the rope there's a chance someone will come along and pull you up, but if you let go, there is no chance of getting pulled up.

Remember, you may be surrounded by everything you want but, not everything you need.

So, I must confess that in the punt return I had against the University of Southern California in 1973, all of the above applied and I was just doing what I loved to do; run with the ball.

The run started just when I realized I didn't know if the return was supposed to be to the right, left or middle. A couple of things about returning punts: 1) A lot of people don't like doing it because the ball is kicked very high and it gives ten maniacs the chance to run down the field full force at you with a bulls-eye on your chest. 2) It sometimes gives the return guy (if he's done it enough) a chance to survey the field and figure out which way the return is going to develop, even if he doesn't know the direction.

So, while the ball was coming down I knew I would have to buy some time until I could see which way the return was supposed to go. I caught the punt on the 48 yard line of the right hash mark and quickly took four strides to the right which put me on the 5 of the fifty yard line. I had no sooner made that move when a few things made me realize I had made the wrong choice: I had already lost two yards by taking those four steps. There were now three USC cover guys in hot pursuit, and I had caught the punt on the short side of the field, which was between the hash marks and the numbers. Putting the sideline in my hip pocket, I was left with no other choice but to head back left. I quickly planted both feet to start this evasive action, but the angle that the Trojan cover guys were taking put a quick end to that plan. Unable to take any steps forward, I knew I had to get a better view to re-evaluate the situation which left me with only one possible direction: backwards.

To say I was "being pursued heavily" is an understatement. I had 3,000 pounds of hostile and mobile USC guys after me, and I was now turned sideways thinking with just my feet and my eyes. Instinctively, my feet kept moving, but remember now, they were moving me backwards! Still trying to find a solution and still moving, I noticed the guys on the USC bench seemed a little bigger *than usual and then I realized it was because I was so close to the sideline. Plus, I had now retreated a total of 12 yards. Nonetheless, I had no choice other than to keep moving; I had to find where the wall was forming.*

A quick analysis of the situation coupled with understanding my own abilities let me know that there was no need to panic; everything was clear. I was still cognizant of what I was capable of doing or not doing, and so I made the most crucial decision; which was to get away from the sideline and get to open field. Then I had to make another decision: could I buy more time? I have retreated 15 yards and counting, and I knew I could not start heading forward just yet. At this juncture frankly a lot of things were running through my mind. I have now back-pedaled close to 20 yards and am making lightening-fast decisions all the while maintaining my confidence in my teammates that they would bring the wall to me; whatever direction it was supposed to be.

I had always wondered if the footwork of Muhammad Ali was something that he would have incorporated into football and I always wanted to see if my decision making came up-to-snuff with "Pistol Pete" Maravich. So, even though these guys weren't football players they were still very influential in my frame of mind and style of play. But, back to the run....

Now we all know the quickest way from point A to point B is a straight line, right? But does that mean it is the only way to get there? Not in my eyes! I backed up more, then went sideways, right and then left, and then the turning point: I did a complete 360! Not a 360 spin, but an actual left, right, left, right in a tight circle. A USC defender grabbed at me, but instead pulled out my mouth piece which turned me back left and I was off to the races.

Lo and behold, my wall had formed to the right and all of the yards I had lost I was gaining back (well, most of them, anyway). My guys are picking off USC would-be-tacklers left and right, like snipers. To see this is a thing of beauty. Just seeing this happen confirms my scenic tour was well worth it. The point being—while it wasn't the quickest path to gain yards, it was a path that ended up with a positive result. We got the job done and caused a little excitement. I didn't limit myself by allowing others to limit my options for me. I set the stage, and others followed. They brought the wall to me.

I didn't know until after the game that I had gone back as far as I had but I knew it was more than 10 yards! I never once thought about just taking the loss. I remember seeing everything slow down and being in a crowd of players, and bodies flying all over the place but I was never convinced I couldn't make positive yardage. You and I can plan and prepare, but there are certain times in our lives when we need to just do!

Spectators saw me backing up and losing yards; I saw the need to back up only to broaden my choices and get a better view of my options. I had to see. I am sure many of the USC Trojan faithful in the stands were delighted to see my "back tracking" and were confident I was going to be tackled for a huge loss. Both sides were seeing the same play, but my view and their view was totally different. Some had already determined I had failed. They may have made that decision in the stands but I hadn't; my teammates who kept blocking for me hadn't; and the Sooner Nation watching on national television back in Oklahoma were probably saying, "What in the hell is he doing?"

You can check out the run on the internet.

Going backward just does not figure into the American mentality. When we think of going "backward" it conjures up all kinds of negative emotions and thoughts. We sometimes joke and use the word to tease an individual who may not be perceived as acting intelligent at that moment; we say, "He's a bit backward." We hear television commentators talk about countries in the world and describe them as "backward" cultures. So, if the term has so many unacceptable connotations to us why in the world would I want you to consider that sometimes you have to go backward before you can go forward?

As a running back, it stands to reason, that at several points and times, you will lose yards. If you see life in a figurative sense as a football game, you will realize that at times you will lose some yardage, too; but that's life. You may not get the anticipated promotion, the starting spot, or the relationship with the one you thought was just the one for you. You may find yourself having to take a step back to get that overall vantage point, before you go forward. In one form or another all of us at some time will lose yardage. Well, it doesn't always mean failure.

Some times things happen to us due to events that are simply out of our control and when that happens, we feel singled out by fate. "Why me?" we ask, "everyone seems happy (or healthy, or rich) but me." That's when we back up and get another perspective to help us figure it out.

There is a difference between a set-back and full-out retreat. Retreating is running away, not wanting to deal with something. You are only thinking of survival. I wasn't retreating that night in '73. I was backing up just enough to view things from a broader scope and possibly see other paths I could take. I had two choices when I caught that punt return: I could guess as to which direction the return was called and go forward and be stopped immediately; or I could go backward, observe how other players were going to react, and see if the right opportunity developed…you know, cause and effect.

Never limit yourself. Thinking "outside the box" will prove innovative and successful time and time again. Those who can institute this gift in the workplace, or those that can master one facet and find another person to master the other facets can still be in the ballgame.

In a game like football, knowing your abilities is critical because you must make split-second decisions that can change the outcome of a game in a moment's time. You've trained years and years in preparation for this, so your muscles react almost without being told; everything becomes instinctive. Life is a slower version of just that. Have you ever had a problem that seemed insurmountable one day and you could not find a solution no matter how hard you tried? Then a day or two later, after you backed up and analyzed the problem from a different angle, maybe even asked people for their opinions, you find the solution?

Retreat signals defeat, but backing up to get a better look indicates intelligence, determination and commitment to move forward when the opportunity arrives. There is a little pride in all of us, but we all have to stop at the gas station now and then to ask for directions.

In the USC punt return I just kept moving. Remember when life sends you backward it's just giving you an opportunity to rethink, refocus, and redo. Keep moving, always keeping in mind where you want to end up. When you think about giving in or giving up, you eliminate the possibility of *any* forward progress.

Millions of fans watching on television probably were disagreeing with what I chose to do that Saturday night, but that doesn't mean I was wrong. Don't lose confidence in what you believe when others don't see the play you see. They are not the one carrying the ball.

Now, did Coach Switzer think I had made the right choice when I started backing up? Maybe not, but the end result was what we both wanted. All of our lives we are coached and prepped to make good choices and wise decisions at the appropriate time. The middle of a play is not the time to be coached. Hallelujah! That's the importance of practice. Do teachers help you during a test? Do doctors look up surgery techniques in the middle of surgery? I hope not. Game time is the time to react with the instilled knowledge and training you have at your disposal. In my case, those years of training filtered down to reactionary movements that were now simply instinctive. They instilled a certain confidence in my abilities.

Even the most successful people at some point have had to make decisions that others question. You can count on it. Life will send you backward at times – layoffs, rejection, illness, family crisis, broken relationships. The key is to know yourself and your abilities. Understand them. Tweak them to peak them (corny but true), but do so with a passion like no other. And remember, we all at sometime need to stop at that gas station.

Confidence comes from hard work that results in internal respect and self-satisfaction: your actions have proven your abilities. Confidence is such an integral part of a person because it impacts the existence of other qualities like determination and poise. It grants you the ability to know and accept your own strengths and weaknesses.

There is a difference in owning a healthy confidence and arrogance. Arrogance comes from thinking you deserve confidence and telling others as much. My wife and I were at a Super Bowl party a few years ago. The host had a great place for a party; televisions everywhere. My wife and I were in a room with several other people away from the larger group. I commented on a play involving a running back and would-be tackler. The situation on the field was one I had found myself in thousands of times. To voice my opinion openly is rare for me, because I usually don't make comments unless asked; or if I know the people and they are *expecting* me to analyze a play. Another guest, who did not know I had played football, told me how incorrect I was and proceeded to tell me why. The surrounding guests grew uncomfortable and one by one flew out of the room (I found out later they went to spread the word about the encounter). It really was funny. The guy thought he had put me in my place.

When he finished, my wife leaned over and asked, "Why did you allow him to talk to you that way?"

I told her I didn't feel the need to say anything in response. The guy's arrogance had allowed him to say far more than he should have and I was pretty certain someone would point that out to him later – someone other than me.

I learned a similar lesson myself as a young teen. There was no chance any of us children in the Washington household were going to be arrogant – it just wasn't allowed. I once was talking to a girl on the telephone and trying to impress her, (I don't have a clue as to what it was I was saying because looking back there was certainly nothing about me that would impress anyone). I turned around and saw my mom with her hands on her hips standing in the doorway just glaring at me. I understood the look. She didn't have to say a word, because as soon as I saw her I was hoping for a hole to crawl in. It seemed as if 20 minutes passed before she finally said, "Junior, we don't do that!"

Backward may be the <u>only</u> way to go until you can go forward

What does that mean? I backed up during that punt return because going forward was not an option at that time. I also backed up because I had confidence in my teammates and myself, and because I was determined to succeed. This confidence came from years of hard work, self-discipline and self awareness. Determination comes from knowing you have a right to be confident. You don't give up, because you have paid the price to be successful. One's belief in himself and internal confidence is what drives his level of determination.

I can name several people, some you know, and others you may not have heard about, who have gotten back up after being knocked down. Look up their stories and you will find that a prerequisite for existing on this planet is the assurance that you *will* get knocked down at times, or find yourself going backward when you want to go forward.

There's Shelia Escovedo, a music artist who had to learn to walk again. Read about Bethany Hamilton, a young lady, 14, who was surfing off the coast of Hawaii when she was attacked by a 14-foot tiger shark, who nearly ate her for lunch. Bethany managed to swim back to shore, but not before the shark had ripped off her left arm. A month after the attack she returned to the water.

The true story of Chris Gardner is an example of someone who had a serious backward run. In 1981, the salesman lost everything he had…his car, his home, bank accounts, his credit cards, and finally his wife. Evicted and forced to live on the streets with his young son he did what most of us would do. He kept trying, kept moving, looking for any opportunity. (That is exactly what I did that day against USC). Finally, he entered the Dean Witter training program to become a stockbroker. During a most difficult time he told his son, "Hey, don't ever let someone tell you, you can't do something – even me. You got a dream – you got to protect it. Some people can't do something themselves so they want to tell you that you can't do it." Gardner eventually became a millionaire through his determined efforts.

Even the most successful people have a backward run now and then, but it is what you do with the set-back that is paramount. You think because you are good or smart, or honest that hard times won't come? They come to everyone in some shape or form at some point. In a football game you can rest assured something bad will happen. Your team is playing well, things are going fine and "BAM!" out of the blue, a fumble, interception, pass interference, a face-mask infraction happens.

If something doesn't go the way you planned, before you retreat, decide how badly you want to make the goal and view it from all angles. This doesn't mean you will get everything you want, but you will be stronger for the attempt.

One of the NFL teams I was fortunate to play for was the Washington Redskins. Before I got there they had been coached at one time by the legendary George Allen. Three things I have heard about Allen; he loved ice cream, practices could be long and hard; and he was a great motivator. His words ring true to us as we learn how we must sometimes go backward before we can go forward. Allen said, "People of mediocre ability sometimes achieve outstanding success because they simply don't know when to quit. Most men succeed because they are determined to."

Never get into a fight with a guy who continues to get up no matter how many times you knock him down. I have always thought defensive players on a football team are the epitome of that quote. If a defensive lineman gets blocked, his will, hustle and sheer determination can overcome that situation to make a play.

We can be that guy.

The Latin phrase *Sapiens ipse fingit fortunam sibi* says it best: *"The wise man creates his destiny himself."* We cannot control the family circumstances into which we were born, the economy, the decisions others make that affect us, but one thing we can control is our own personal choices. Our lives are nothing more than a combination of many tiny moment-by-moment choices that have life long consequences.

Many find themselves in less than desirable situations (losing yardage), because of their own doing. No one was chasing them to cause them to lose yards or caused them to fumble; they ran back there and dropped the ball all by themselves! Think about how one small indiscretion can change an entire life. We have all heard stories of young, promising athletes, musicians, intellectuals, or even everyday "Joes," who have wonderful opportunities ahead, yet make one poor choice that either ruins their career or impacts their reputation forever.

Again, there is no guarantee for anything, but keeping your mind on the goal (the end zone) is so important for success; it increases your chances. Ask often, "Could this one decision keep me from obtaining any of my dreams, my goals?"

I can't recall pulling for many football teams coached by Lou Holtz, but I love these words attributed to Coach Holtz:

"The answers to these questions can play a role in your success or failure:

1) Can people trust me to do what's right?
2) Am I committed to doing my best?
3) Do I care about other people and show it?

If your answer is 'yes' to these questions, you'll stand a good chance of being a better person."

I suppose going backward can produce an exciting challenge at times. Really though, how in the world could anyone enjoy losing yardage, going through the hard times? Believe me it can be stressful and a bit hard on your nerves. I have been there both on and off the field. But, believe it or not, there are some rare folks (never intended for success) who enjoy the attention, the sympathy, the built in excuse that life is not fair. And when the game requires a backward run now and then, they would much rather take the easy way out and blame someone else. We all have done it; find others to blame for our own shortcomings. I have heard a million excuses:

"I missed it because the quarterback threw the ball behind me." "My linemen suck." "I never had a chance – they blitzed me from the weak side." "The Coach's game plan sucked." The finger pointing is just one characteristic of how some react when life's events send them backwards for a time.

Some of us are ill-prepared and have plenty of excuses when life is challenging. They come to the game unprepared for the contest and when the going gets tough they are ready to pull out the white flag.

Successful people take responsibility for their own actions. They see something like the USC punt return run as an anomaly, a learning experience, a temporary set back; only a springboard for bringing them closer to success.

Another trait I have observed in successful world class athletes is the ability to change and adapt in negative situations. They are always willing to try something else if the situation warrants it. Winners believe they can make positive yardage regardless of how far they go backwards; others just *hope* they can. That isn't cockiness; it is a firm self confidence that says, "I will not stop trying until the ref blows his whistle."

President Roosevelt authored thoughts that have inspired people for generations – the words still empower us today:

> *"It is not the critic who counts;*
> *not the man who points out how the strong man stumbles,*
> *or where the doer of deeds could have done them better.*
> *The credit belongs to the man who is actually in the arena,*
> *whose face is marred by dust and sweat and blood;*
> *who strives valiantly; who errs, who comes short again and*
>   *again,*
> *because there is no effort without error and shortcoming;*
> *but who does actually strive to do the deeds;*
> *who knows great enthusiasms, the great devotions;*
> *who spends himself in a worthy cause; who at the best knows*
>   *in the end*
> *the triumph of high achievement, and who at the worst,*
> *if he fails, at least fails while daring greatly,*
> *so that his place shall never be with those cold and timid souls*
> *who neither know victory nor defeat."*

It is very important that you don't allow the negative opinion of others to infiltrate your mind to the extent that you question your own abilities. The opinion of others should matter, but own the power to react or not react to those opinions. I like to think of negative opinions as both an opportunity to improve myself, and, or a challenge to change someone's opinion. We can't just live in a cocoon, we need to be aware of other opinions.

You may not know the name of Eddie Arcaro – he was the only jockey in history to win five Kentucky Derbies, six Belmont Stakes and six Preakness Stakes. He ended his career with over 5,000 wins, but there's another part to the story. He lost 250 consecutive races when he first started. I'm sure there were times he felt like his horse was running backward, but passion for his sport and believing in his dreams drove him on to realize a long and prosperous career.

The first eight years of my ten year NFL career goes like this: 5-11, 5-11, 7-9, 7-9, 6-8, a whopping 8-8; and then two consecutive Super Bowls!

If you want to measure a person's character, look closely at the times when they have had to overcome adversity, obstacles, and pain. The separation point of winners and losers is how they think and what they do when life sends them backward. I value the punt return I had against USC because I know the price I paid to gain those hard yards. The pay value was worth it–every twisting motion, every switch of direction, every defender I had to shake off–all had a part in creating for me a moment when running backward was hailed as something magical.

And then...

When the dust settled, I knew I was somewhere close to where I had originally started this journey and at this point, I am really winded. As I am leaving the field, the crowd was buzzing and the first person I saw was my backfield coach, Coach Wendell Mosley. He greets me with a jaw full of tobacco and a grin as wide as the football field. Coach Switzer was next and I can tell he's suppressing a smile and that he feels he needs to reprimand me, but, by the time he finishes telling me not to do that again, he's grinning, too.

JOE WASHINGTON

Sometimes, backward can indeed be forward. I learned a lot that night. We were going to be a great football team with great players. I learned my teammates would never quit on me and they would continue to come to my rescue. By the way, the game ended in a 7 – 7 tie. USC was lucky to tie and they know it to this day!

—Joe

SECRET #3

It Isn't Always About Winning or is It?

Kim, (my younger brother) and I were the coach's kids who loved everything about football. Because we were coach's kids we thought the game couldn't exist without us and we understood every aspect of the game as well as any other person on the planet by the time we were in elementary school. Kim understood these things at an even earlier age than I did. We understood that every person's job concerning the team was important and contributed to its success. It didn't matter what that person's responsibility was; if he was around the team, he was important.

We loved being around and interacting with the older football players and were willing to do just about anything as long as we could be out on the field with them. This included practice, of course, but it also meant being involved in real games, too. So, instead of sitting in the stands with Mom and Pat, our sister, we were down on the field, "working hard". (Not really, it was pure fun personified!)

We appointed ourselves in charge of whatever was needed because we could do it all; adjust equipment, "gofer" this and "gofer" that, tape ankles, give massages; we were always in the middle of things. Well, when push came to shove, the self proclaimed title we gave ourselves was trainers, despite the fact most fans would have called us water boys.

One of our many responsibilities was to rush out onto the field during timeouts with water and towels to wipe the sweat off the players' hands, arms, faces, and heads. Mom got us some white overalls we wore with the team name "Panthers" printed on the back. We thought that was the coolest thing ever. And, we wore football shoes with real cleats, just in case we needed to make a quick cut or something. We took the job seriously, and we were focused; focused as a man juggling knives! We were committed to our duties until the final whistle blew; the score took second fiddle.

In Port Arthur, as in most every big or small town across Texas, high school football games were played on Friday nights, under the lights. Games played in the humid Texas heat guaranteed that every player would need a towel most every break. Even when the weather turned cooler and a chill was in the air, the football players would be sweating under their helmets and pads.

Kim and I would run out loaded down with towels and then "it" would happen. As the players, usually down on one knee in the huddle, began to remove their helmets, body heat would be released from their heads and send swirls of steam rising upwards. To us, the rising steam was a special anointing, a verification that these were real football players, playing hard, getting the job done. We ran as fast as we could toward those steaming heads to offer relief; we wanted to be in the midst of that sacred mist.

When I first started playing football for my dad in the ninth grade, Kim, younger by two years, was still coming out on the field offering those towels. Because I was now on the team, our best friend, Arthur Criswell, whom we called, "Onion" took over my towel duty. Onion also understood the creed; the code. During one of the first October games, a timeout was called and I took my helmet off, then quickly turned to my brother. I didn't have to say a word. Kim and Onion were on the same page.

Kim looked at me; then with a huge smile he mouthed excitedly, "Yeah, Joe, your head's steamin', your head's steamin!'"

I couldn't let on how happy I was; it was the middle of the game, but Kim knew. It was a huge confirmation to me that I had arrived. I was a real football player.

In that slice of precious time, it wasn't about beating other players or always winning. I was in the circle on one knee in the "mist;" elated that I was getting to do what I loved. The fact that my head was steaming was proof I was legit - giving it my all; working hard to compete. I loved playing football, but I knew I wouldn't always win. We were taught:

If you lose, make sure you don't quit.

Play as hard as you can.

Do the best you can and enjoy every minute until the final whistle blows and the game ends.

We were told to be honest when critiquing our performance and take away something positive from every game. Win or lose we loved the game; I still do.

"It isn't always about winning ... ." Well, of course it is! Winning is the benchmark everyone strives to reach. Winning is a common goal, obtainment of which slowly whittles out the lesser opponent until only one is left standing. Winning equates the best. Winning equates success. Winning equates fulfillment. Without a winner, we wouldn't have competition and without competition we would only have complacency, and with complacency comes stagnation; no growth, no development, no improvement, no furtherance.

From the moment you are born, life becomes all about winning. Winning the struggle to survive infancy; winning the attention of parents over a sibling, winning the battle between adolescence and adulthood, and winning the battle to succeed. It's life. In sports, there will only be one winner at the end of the season. People are just innately trying to win.

So, it really always *is* about winning and the old cliché, "It isn't if you win or lose, but how you play the game," clearly resulted from someone trying to make all of the losers feel better. Let's face it, there is only ONE winner but multiple losers, so losers are usually the masses, and we don't want the masses feeling incompetent.

That said, allow me to add, it isn't always ALL about winning. It isn't always ONLY about winning. It isn't only the winner who takes something from the competition. It isn't only the winner who walks away a better person.

Winning means different things to different people. "Steamin' heads" meant something to my brother and me at that stage of our lives. It was the first step to our success.

We knew that once we were part of the "sacred mist", we had made it and our dreams were coming true! We knew it was our beginning. It meant more to me than winning a Super Bowl ring because it was something I shared with my side-shadow, my brother; the only person who shared my every thought and every goal from beginning to end. No one else would have understood.

Think about what losing does for us. I've always said, losing is the training ground to winning. As painful as losing is, it can provide unprecedented enlightenment. "You take a line away from a win, but you take a book away from a loss," wrote Paul Brown, legendary NFL coach. Losing is what makes us better persons, a better society, a better nation and a better world. There has to be a loser in every competition and competition forces development.

If everyone won, there would be no challenge for improvement; no need for change or growth. We wouldn't have to analyze our performance to determine where it needed improvement. Some of my most elusive moves are a result of a loss, because I was so bothered by the fact that someone covered me on a pass route, I would replay the route in my mind over and over, every step I made, every step my opponent made, and the rest of the defense, too. Then I would imagine a different move here, a move there, or a hurdle over the opponent. I would run the play again and again until I found what I needed to accomplish the desired outcome.

This is true for any "loser" who wants to remain in the game, whether the game be a sport or profession. Staying in the game demands that losers analyze themselves, set their egos aside and honestly critique themselves; then make the necessary adjustments. Gee, just check your own effort. Losing, in some cases (only some) isn't bad; it is just a part of life.

Don't let being labeled with a loss make you afraid of going out there and laying it on the line. Don't let the idea of losing, paralyze or compromise your confidence and ability to perform at the highest level next time. No one wins every game, every time. No baseball player, living or passed, hit a home run, or got a base hit for that matter, every time he stepped to the plate. Even the great Babe Ruth, "King of Swat", struck out 1,330 times.

Even though I loved football, I had some difficult days. One hit I recall while playing with the Baltimore Colts rattled me so badly and hurt so much, it brought tears to my eyes. He caught me looking up over my left shoulder for a pass and hit me under my chin right above my numbers. He cleaned my clock, darn near killed me. My feet came off the ground and they were higher up than my head for a while. When I did hit the ground, it was the back of my head first, my butt, then the heels of my feet. I was not having fun at *that* moment. I was just trying to move something … anything … an eyelash. I thought I was dead; I couldn't move. All I could see was a fog, a cloudy mist above me, and it was not the "anointed mist" I spoke of earlier. The figure peering down at me was Tom Darden, with the Cleveland Browns. He had hit me and it was so bad, Tom knelt down next to me and asked, "Little Joe, you okay?"

I was not okay. In fact, I wanted to take my uniform off at that very moment and go home! Even though we won that game, I wasn't overly excited about it. I didn't give a hoot who won or lost at that moment.

No one enjoys a sport or even his life *all* the time. At some point, everyone experiences a disappointment, a loss. Failure is not who we are, failure is an event. My point is this: the reality of what makes the world go around is the possibility of winning, but there is no such thing in life as winning all the time. So what does this mean? The human race needs life skills to understand winning and losing is as much a part of life as eating and sleeping. It shouldn't always be about winning, as the chapter title suggests. Does this mean we shouldn't teach our youngsters to give their full effort in order to win? No, but how can you tell a kid who gave his best effort that he didn't succeed because he didn't win according to the scoreboard? Both winning and losing have to be kept to a level perspective. You can't get too high when you win, nor, get too low when you lose.

Different stages in our lives usually determine our willingness to accept a loss. In the beginning, when kids start playing organized sports, everyone is treated equally. All the children have equal playing time in order to develop their skills, learn the rules of the game and figure out what comes most naturally to them; a loss or a win is not the focus of the game as everyone is learning. This is really the only time that it isn't about winning. As the stages of the game evolve, the level of competition is defined and individual skills become more evident. The first thing that goes is equal playing time for each player. Before you know it, tryouts are the only way to make a team; some players will make it, some won't.

The same is true in academics. Instead of winning a game trophy, a student may win a certificate of achievement, or the highest grade in the class, or recognition by their peers. The same applies to the world of business, too. All strive to be the best at their profession. Whether we are the player on the field, the coach of the team, the parent in the stands, the teacher in the classroom, or CEO of a company, we want to win. We aspire to be better than our peers or competition.

But, for every win, there will be a loss, and with every loss there will be disappointment. How you manage that loss will make the difference between a loss and thinking of yourself as a loser.

Think about how winning and losing determine the paths we choose. It is innate to want to win and each of us will instinctively focus on using whatever trait that comes most naturally to us individually to strive toward that goal. The child who can easily accept losing a football game might be the same child who cannot accept being the number two student in his class. I really believe an individual's winning mindset is determined by what comes most naturally to them. When you should be concerned is when it isn't about winning, at anything. If you truly don't care, then you have accepted complacency and mediocrity?

As a competitor, one of the greatest foes we battle and one that requires more energy than leaving the refrigerator door open, is complacency. Sometimes even winning and being successful on a consistent basis can be the main ingredient for complacency. The effort it takes to win on a consistent level is daunting. This shouldn't be anything that alarms us. It's just human nature to become satisfied or content with past actions or accomplishments when we aren't individually challenged.

Our instinctive beliefs guide our paths of action or non-action in dealing with complacency. Some complacent people believe there is such a thing as being perfect and they are; so they never strive to become better; they are as close to perfect as you can get. However, most complacent people, are the opposite. For them, there is no such thing as perfect, so they say, "Ah, what the heck. I'm just fine with doing what I do to get by."

A coach I knew over the years, who was a Sooner, then Texas coach and Athletic Director, Darrell Royal, stated in the book, *Conversations with a Football Legend (2006)*, "It got so that winning wasn't exciting and losing became intolerable ... climbing is a thrill ... maintaining is a bitch."

A former University of Oklahoma football coach, the great Bud Wilkinson said, "Complacency is the greatest enemy of success." Once you have reached a goal it takes even greater effort to maintain your place at the top. I guess Bud would know a little about staying at the top. He led the Sooners to that 47 game winning streak, which is still the record today!

I really think that it is what we take away from any loss that's important. The key is to still see the possibility of a win within your grasp following a loss; to believe that you can still climb that steep mountain again to become a winner.

In my senior year at Oklahoma, 1975, the season started out with us being ranked number one as defending National

Champions. We'd gone through our schedule undefeated, winning and covering most anticipated spreads. Next up, Kansas at home. Older fans remember it well. Needless to say, we lost the game. I was shocked, but probably more pissed than anything else. We all were. In four years at Oklahoma I had only experienced one other loss and that had been three years earlier in my freshman year.

We made our way into the locker room, but that day the room was like walking into a morgue. No celebrating – nothing. It was lifeless. Some of us tried to play it off as if it were just another part of life, but as seniors this was not how it was supposed to be, nor how we wanted to leave our mark at the university. I'm pretty sure the air had been sucked out of the whole stadium.

We all did some soul searching that day there in our own dressing room. For a lot of the players, this was their first time to lose in an OU uniform. I recall Coach Switzer's words to this day. "You have nothing to be ashamed of," he said. "You've ridden this gravy train for a long time."

Those were the words you'd expect from Coach, but they didn't make you feel any better. We didn't want to leave the locker room and hear any words of solace, or anyone asking, "Are you okay?" And we surely didn't want to go out there and smile and be a good sport. We didn't want to be comforted and didn't want to have to comfort anyone else! We just wanted to sit there and not move, because movement somehow meant acceptance.

After licking my wounds and replaying the game to understand what took place, I knew what my teammates expected of me. My upbringing as a coach's son helped me know exactly what needed to be done. I knew that how we practiced that next week for the upcoming game was crucial. I knew that the intensity level of practice would have to be cranked up a few notches and it would include everyone. We were at a crossroad. Our winning streak had just been broken, and now there was a chance we wouldn't win the conference championship and our national championship hopes were looking bleak. In order to be prepared to have a chance against Missouri the following week, we had an intense practice schedule ahead of us.

Missouri was always a tough opponent, especially defensively. We had won each contest with them over the previous three years, but physically they would always beat us to hell! Especially, *my* little hiney. We had to play there and everyone would be watching to see if the Kansas loss had broken our spirit along with breaking our winning streak.

Initially, during the game, we looked like our usual powerful, unbeatable selves and went in at halftime with a 20 to 0 lead. But, in the second half, as happens in most football games, there came a point in time when things began to go bad. The difference in the good athletes and the ones that aren't as good is how the good ones handle the bad spell without panic. With three and half minutes left in the final quarter, we didn't handle it like the Oklahoma team we were.

We found ourselves down 20–27 with barely three minutes left in the game. It was fourth and one on our own 22-yard line when time-out was called. Steve Davis, our Baptist minister quarterback went to the sideline to talk to the coaches about what we were going to do and what we were going to run. As Steve was on the sideline conversing with the coaches to get the correct play, we were all standing in the huddle knowing and understanding that it is a defining moment in all of our careers at the University of Oklahoma. Are we going to do the unthinkable ... lose two games in a row? No one said a word. I say nothing, the linemen say nothing, not even the little fly flying around in the huddle made a buzz. We just stood silently wondering what play would be called. I was wishing and hoping and praying that my number would be called and that I would get the ball. But for some reason, I was thinking, I probably wouldn't.

Steve came in to take his position in the huddle which was right next to me. Even before he stepped into the huddle he said, "Little Joe, be ready."

I exhaled with relief because I knew then they were calling my play. Steve stepped in and called it then we walked to the line of scrimmage. I could see our linemen approach the line and they had regained their spring and bounce; an arrogance they had always had before the Kansas game. I suppose "swagger" is what they call it now.

I remember getting into my stance and being conscious of my feet and hand position so that when the ball was snapped to Steve, I could explode out of the stance with speed. As I took the first seven steps, I gathered myself, got my emotions under control, to receive the anticipated pitch from Steve. Back-side I know Chez Evans and Karl Baldischweir are reach-blocking toward where the play is being run. I can also see the whole right side of our offense move into position to perform their responsibilities. Right tackle, Mike Vaughan and Terry Webb, right guard, perform their normal veer-blocking duties. Dennis Buchanan snapped the ball then reached their backside defensive tackle. Then, Jim Littrell, fullback, faked taking the handoff and went through his blocking assignment. Elvis Peacock lead-blocks as he has done so many times during the season, unselfishly. Our tight end, Victor Hicks, instead of bumping the linebacker who is covering him and releasing him to take their safety, bumps the linebacker then releases laterally outside to block out the supporting cornerback that has been the support man for the pitch, but he wasn't expecting the change in the blocking scheme.

Then, Steve pitched the ball to me. I caught it, took two steps, planted and stepped behind Victor Hicks' shield on the unsuspecting charging cornerback and I knew I had the one yard we needed for the first down. But at this point, I'm still seeing daylight and I take another three steps and plant my right foot and head back left against the grain. At this time, Jim Littrell is downfield and Tinker Owens from the far left side has somehow made his way downfield so I cut behind both of them. As I cut behind both of them, I start thinking, "I might be able to take this to the house!" Seventy yards later, you could hear, in the words of Billy Sims, "A rat piss on cotton," in that stadium.

We were now behind 27–26. We could easily kick the extra point to tie the game, but that was not in the Sooner DNA. We called time-out again. Steve approached the huddle again with the play. And it's my number again and the same play! I am a little concerned about running this play again only because we were now in the shaded part of the field and the grass where I would be trying to maneuver was slick from the humidity and the sun was setting. Plus, I had just run 78 yards. But, I thought, "Well, we will see what happens."

The ball is snapped, then again Steve pitches it to me. I cut in again behind Victor Hicks' shield and jump the last three yards into the end zone. Of course, Missouri players were jumping around, all feeling that I hadn't scored, but, as I've said thousands of times – even Ray Charles, Ronnie Milsap, and Stevie Wonder could tell you I scored.

Those were some two weeks. Had we become complacent? Had Kansas made its changes and met its challenges? Maybe a little of both. Sure, the loss stung, but we recovered and moved on to win a back to back national championship. I honestly never felt like a loser because of that loss.

One quote from the legendary coach, Vince Lombardi, is often misquoted. Most cite him as stating, "Winning isn't everything, it is the *only* thing." Lombardi actually said, *"Winning isn't everything, but making the effort to win is."* Do your best. There is an unmistakable pride in going full out and doing it with a lot of heart, even in defeat. The score may indicate a loss, but you may have won a personal or collective victory, and that provides a platform to build on, which can be just as important. Don't get me wrong; losing still sucks, and the feeling is unexplainable but mature players understand that a loss provides valuable lessons for success in the future. Maturity is key to handling both winning and losing.

This can be applied to any business, venture, or organization. Great competitors never throw in the towel, give up, or check out. You attain success by leaving it all on the field. The legendary UCLA basketball coach, John Wooden taught players his *Pyramid of Success* principles, which urged players to stop looking at the scoreboard; just play hard until the final whistle. I thought about attending UCLA just to be in the same atmosphere as Coach Wooden.

Winning has to have a balance. It takes more courage to face everyday personal battles than an opponent on a football field. So, try your best to do your best. Enjoy the contest, work hard to get through the hardest of days, and do it the way it should be done. When you do, no more can be asked or expected.

And then…

Some retired pros say they never watch football; they don't follow any team. I can understand not following a specific team but I can't understand not having any interest. Not only do I make every University of Oklahoma game possible, I follow pro teams, still enjoying my favorites. This is funny I know, but I even follow some because of my love for certain uniforms worn by teams: the Redskins' maroon pants with gold and white stripes, the Bears' dark pants with white socks and white shoes, the San Diego Chargers' uniforms with the lightning bolt on the side of their pants. I follow the Broncos and Giants because I like the Mannings; the brothers seem to have a good relationship. I am partial to any brother act because of my relationship with my brother. I like their dad, Archie – what a cool guy.

Then, I follow some teams because of some personal connection. There are some pro coaches whom I met along the way, and there are guys I played with who are now coaching; so we stay in touch. I also like to watch teams who have great running backs.

Speaking of loving a team, something very special happens when a community comes together to support a sports team. I have lived in Baltimore since playing for the "Baltimore" Colts starting in 1978. As a kid, I was a huge fan of the Baltimore Colts and after arriving here I discovered that many Colts, some I idolized as a kid, had put down roots here. I had the opportunity to meet many of those childhood heroes. I was privileged to have some great teammates here; Roosevelt Leeks, Bert Jones, Don McCauley and I really grew to appreciate Coach Ted Marchibroda. By the way, we moved to Baltimore when there was 26 inches of snow on the ground.

The city embraced the Colts and me. Even when I left to play for the Redskins in 1981 I missed the special camaraderie Baltimore exhibited for the team. Many probably expected me to move back to Texas or Oklahoma after retiring from football and I never thought I would be settling on the east coast, but my wife and I decided to build our home and raise our daughter here, because it just felt right, comfortable and accepting. In fact, a nick-name for Baltimore is "Small-timore" because it feels like small town USA even though it is a thriving big city. There is also easy access to trains and airports, plus, we are within driving distance from Washington, D.C, and New York City, too.

We love the "Little Italy" area of town and have favorite restaurants there. We also frequent some great Baltimore restaurants that serve the best seafood anywhere. The parks, museums, all the sports teams, and a revitalized downtown give visitors a taste of the unique and cultural blend of the city.

But, it is the Baltimore sports fans I especially appreciate. We were devastated when the Colts were stolen away overnight and moved to Indianapolis in 1984. In fact, some fans are still embittered over the deal. To this day when many fans think of the Colts they still think of the old Baltimore team and players like Johnny Unitas, Lenny Moore, Art Donovan, and Raymond Berry.

After deep disappointment, Baltimore fans perked up twelve years later when another NFL team relocated to Baltimore from Cleveland. The new team was named the Ravens, in honor of the poem by famous writer, Edgar Allen Poe, who was himself a Baltimore resident for a time. The Ravens are now one of the most valuable sports franchises in the world.

By the way, the Washington Redskins organization was wonderful to work for, too. Redskins fans are die-hard and to be in that atmosphere was something I will treasure for a lifetime.

A few years back, the Ravens were getting ready for the playoff game with the Pittsburg Steelers, and the whole city was impacted. City statues were painted purple and white, Ravens' shirts and hats were everywhere and the upcoming game was being talked about on the streets, in cabs, and in every business or restaurant. It is fun to be part of that and another reason we love our adopted hometown.

The same wonderful thing takes place in every small town all across America on Friday nights during football season, and it sure takes place in Norman when a big game is coming up for OU. The community is involved and everyone is eager for the contest.

The spirit of competition is everywhere and the entire community benefits.

Some athletes don't realize how many people are supporting them, living each moment of the game with them, committing to the team no matter what. The beauty of team sports is found in the fans who are a big part of any team's success; they are the ones in the stands who believe in you. I liked playing in front of thousands of fans, but I would have played on a vacant lot, or, behind a barn with no one watching and enjoyed it just as much. Why? Because it was how I started and because it was about more than winning; (even though the feeling of winning is quite unexplainable because of what goes into it) it was the joy of the game itself.

The final game of my college career was against Michigan at the Orange Bowl in Florida. As fate would have it, we would be playing for our second National Championship. Even though there was a lot at stake for whoever won that night, winning wasn't the only thing on my mind. There was a lot to reflect on or about. The Michigan game was emotionally taxing for a lot of reasons, besides being a bowl game and my last game as a Sooner. There was the added hype of being a Heisman Trophy candidate, and playing through a myriad of injuries. I had set a lot of goals; some accomplished, but most not. We went out to fight a hard-fought battle against Michigan that night and came out with a 14-6 win and our second national title!

After the final whistle blew and while sitting in that locker room alone in my thoughts, it really hit me. It ain't just about winning. That game authenticated our careers, created a bond that exists among us teammates to this day. Sure, reaching personal goals is important, but the team's goals came first and the whole team shared the joy and magic of that moment.

Yes, I still love football! It was and still is a large part of my life. It taught me to love and respect this life. Nowhere is the realization of a person's mortality so true or clearer than in the life of a professional athlete. Father time is only SO generous when it comes to providing a window to be physically able to perform on the field. I still think about those long twisting runs, the championships, but most of all I remember my teammates who have become lifelong friends, confirming that it is about more than winning. Replaying the games in my mind is no different than anyone remembering high moments and low moments in life; moments we all experience. I know I was blessed to play and work at something I loved.

My definition of losing is simply this; you didn't win. Whatever your current game happens to be, whether it is a job or school, or sports – the ultimate goal is to succeed. At that point nothing else matters other than creating and focusing your energies and effort to reach that goal. But, remember success may come in various forms. Just get into the game, inspire, encourage, and be a component of change, and a great competitor whether you win or lose. Enjoy the journey, pay attention to the trees you walk past (enjoy the forest and the trees). In other words, enjoy every day of your life and always do your best: it all passes way too fast.

—Joe

SECRET #4

Credit: Be Secure Enough to Give It – Insecure Enough to Not Expect It

As I approach a hundred years old, I am convinced that our attitudes, our behavior, our prejudices, or lack thereof, are learned and dictated by the environment in which we are nurtured. We are basically born with no prejudices. We are born needy, pretty much waiting for someone else to mold and take care of us, not caring who does it or how. If you are taken from birth from your natural mother who believed that two and two equals four, and given to a mother that believed that two and two equals six, you would grow up believing just that. You would take on her attitude; she would influence you and your opinions. Simple, really—we are what we are exposed to. Just like the adage goes: children live what they learn.

Hopefully by now I've made it clear that I know I didn't get here on my own. My dad, my mom, my brother, my sister, my coaches, my teammates, my universe all made me who I am.

Those of us who can accept the reality that life is not an I, I, I, me, me, me world have been nourished and cared for in an unselfish environment of individuals comfortable with giving credit and acknowledging the opinions of others.

I was exposed to a lot of opinions as a kid, but equally sheltered from the vast reality that existed in the 1950's and 60's. For the most part, especially with my mom, I always had options. Very few things were etched out in black and white, right and wrong, and yes and no. There seemed to be something worthwhile in everything and everybody to give credit or credence to if you took the time to take note of it.

We are a world of influences. It is an innate action for us to help others. We, as people, just naturally look to lend a hand. There has been some influence in our lives that caused us to believe that we should be kind. It is a natural instinct to take care of your own needs and others and we usually rise to the occasion when someone else is in need. But the selfish factions that are me, me, me, I, I, I apply that relentless peer pressure that we all incur, changing our innocent, unassuming caring character into non team members who think every man is an island. By giving credit to those who have helped us in even the most minute of circumstances we are validating our existence; one of the reasons we exist in this world. We all play roles, whether significant or small, realizing that we do need others and there is nothing wrong with letting it be known. What we are talking about here is the simple action of consideration and being considerate, which essentially goes hand and hand with giving and receiving credit.

Youngsters have the tendency to take their parents, teachers, family members, friends, etc. for granted, mainly, I believe, because they have not yet had to be the caregiver; thus have not had to organize their lives to meet anyone's needs but their own (not to mention that they think they know everything). There is a period, however, when the reality of the importance of those who have influenced us hits home and we see clearly we are a product of our environment. For some, it comes at a moment when a situation arises and some vivid advice or teaching comes to mind and the realization comes to us that we don't know everything and Mom and Dad were pretty smart after all.

There we were, headed off to college. I was driving my high school teammate, Glenn Comeaux, and me up to Norman, Oklahoma. He and I would be roommates at the University of Oklahoma and both play football for the Sooners. Seemed like a dream. The farther away we got from my hometown, the more it hit me. I was leaving every person who had always been there for me: my dad and mom, my brother and sister, and the coaches, teachers, teammates, and friends who had encouraged me.

About 70 miles from town, I blinked back a few tears before Glenn could see, then I saw him wiping something from his eyes, too. Soon, we both were bawlin' like babies. We were two young men who suddenly realized we were on our own—or actually much worse, depending on each other. And we were entering a new phase of life from which we would never return; that phase called adulthood.

We didn't say a word; I just kept driving, thinking, Glenn and I are roommates, Glenn and I are depending on each other, Glenn and I are driving seven hours to Oklahoma and the last thing his mother told me in private was, "Whatever you do, don't let Glenn, under any circumstances, drive."

I had been driving six hours straight and it was now after midnight. I was feeling the effects of the long drive and the emotions Glenn and I brought on this road trip to adulthood. By now I want to sleep, so the obvious thing for me to do is let Glenn drive, but wait, the last thing Glenn's mom told me before we left was whatever I do don't let Glenn drive. Well, to keep that from happening I pulled over on the side of the road from time to time to run wind sprints on the side of the road to keep myself awake. You can imagine what those 18-wheel drivers on Interstate 35 thought seeing me on the side of the road running wind sprints at 1 o'clock in the morning. After about three stops and ten sprints later, I couldn't take it anymore. I had to sleep or we'd end up over a cliff somewhere. I silently asked Mrs. Comeaux for forgiveness and asked Glenn to drive. I had an orange Plymouth Duster Twister at the time. I was 5'9" about 165 pounds and Glenn was 6'1" and weighed in around 220 pounds at the time. We switched sides and I got in and hooked my seat belt to finally get some rest. Because Glenn was a little taller I just naturally anticipated his readjusting the seat and mirrors. Well, he did none of the above. He grabbed the steering wheel with both hands, sitting tensely upright with his chin between his hands nearly touching the steering wheel. Now, I am wide awake and he then spins the tires with gravel popping all around the car, never even looking over his shoulder to enter the freeway. Needless to say I didn't sleep a wink the next five minutes before I took the wheel again. I was wiped out by the time we reached the Norman city limit sign.

I knew my family would visit Norman and see my games, but that didn't keep me from having those unsettling moments when I knew nothing would ever be the same. I realized at a very young age that growing up wasn't all it was cracked up to be, and I would come to wonder why anybody would want to grow up, anyway. I know I didn't want to. Why would I want that?

I understood even at that age how good I had it as a kid; keys to the gym, play all day, swim all day during the summer, three squares and no responsibility. A lot of people were responsible for me being in that secure position. I even credit the lady who used to sit on her porch and call the parents of the kids who she thought were getting out of line. Lord only knows how many times she saved me from myself. Why would I want to grow up? I was insulated by a world of people who cared, guided, nourished, and influenced me.

I had seen my father every day of my life. As mentioned, I rode to school with him every morning and then saw him later each afternoon on the practice field. My mom and my sister, Pat, were also there for anything and everything I needed, even without my knowing it was needed. Mom and Pat were as consistent as daylight. Pat was the defender of the family name, no matter what, and the one who'd take on what little responsibilities her brothers had so they could go and do their thing. She would always cover for us.

Because of my family's willingness to support one another I was free to pursue whatever I wanted. I had lived my dream at a very early age. But this one dream was a constant focus of my childhood: a dream of playing on my dad's team with my lifelong buddy and roommate, my brother Kim. I was the older brother, but Kim's maturity and even-natured attitude enabled me to not focus so much on being the big brother and allowed me to just enjoy having my brother around. When we stepped into the huddle and he *called the plays the big brother-little brother identity disappeared. As a sophomore, Kim's leadership and unbelievable skills as our quarterback, were the missing ingredients our football teams had longed for. I rushed for a lot of yards, but he was the reason for the wins. He was our Johnny Unitas, # 19.*

I remember my childhood as a time of joy and being in an environment where you played every day, but I also remember that environment producing characters and incidents that you never forgot and are always relating to.

The movie *Sandlot* reminds me of my childhood, and all the pickup games we played in every sport you could imagine and then some. We learned to get along and work out our differences; you had to, if you were going to play together every day, you needed everybody to show up so that you wouldn't be short on people. Playing with and being together with these kids, I learned to be considerate by making a serious effort to put myself in their shoes when there were disagreements, allowing me to realize there's always a solution. These were influencing relationships, and I now realize I wouldn't be who I am today without them. I wonder where all those kids are, how they look, and if they are okay.

It would be difficult not to mention the most important person at OU who helped me transition to university life. That one person without a doubt was my backfield coach who recruited me, Coach Wendell Mosley. He talked often about what he had imagined for me and what he thought I would be able to accomplish. He was always upbeat. I always thought he had the easiest and the toughest job on the planet, coaching a bunch of the most talented backs in the country.

Once, I was sitting in his office waiting to talk to him while he was on the phone talking to Coach Bear Bryant, the legendary coach at Alabama. I sat there listening to Coach Mosley tell Coach Bryant that he'd love to come to Alabama during the offseason and give them a few pointers on the wishbone. As I sat there, a gentleman stuck his head in the door several times trying to get the coach's attention.

Finally Coach Mosley told Coach Bryant to hold for a second. I actually heard him say, "Hold on a second, Bear." He then put his hand over the mouthpiece of the phone and asked the man, "Sir, may I help you?"

And the guy replied, "Coach, I am here to connect your phone."

Coach Moseley laughed harder than I did. Funny thing, every other back at Oklahoma tells the same story, only they were the guys sitting listening to Coach Mosley talking to Bear Bryant.

The man really believed in me. I miss him.

I am also still mourning the recent passing of Coach Gene Hochevar. He was my offensive line coach at Oklahoma in my sophomore, junior, and senior years. Most offensive line coaches are pretty groovy guys. He was a good man and great coach. He really got to know his players, and practices were intense, to say the least. He prepared them for a physical game-time but they had fun, most of the time. The art of line play, especially his philosophy on short yardage and goal line play for lineman, was really the core of our offensive strength.

Coach Hochevar was only sixty-eight years old when he passed away. He too, will be greatly missed.

There were also a host of teammates who impacted me every day. Again, the great Greg Pruitt set the bar high for me and any other back who wanted to be a part of the great tradition of OU running backs. I was proud of Greg's accomplishments because we were close in size and he hailed from the same part of Texas (we are actually distant relatives some kind of way). I got to know Steve Owens (whom I now consider a good friend) and would get to meet players like Billy Vessels who played on some of the greatest OU teams ever in the '50's. Jakie Sandefer, a great Sooner running back in the 50's who not only bleeds crimson but he bleeds crimson with the OU initials in it. He's a man with a huge heart and I love him ("Pal") to death. You have got to tip your hat to these guys, some I didn't mention but they are the ones responsible for creating that massive foundation and tradition that exists today and gives Oklahoma its unique place in collegiate annals.

Those who are not concerned about getting the credit realize that all of life is a team sport. We matter to each other, whether we want to admit it or not. We need each other, to go to bat for each other, and have one another's back. "No man is an island…."

After one of our games during my sophomore year, the three team captains pulled me into Coach Switzer's office and asked him why he hadn't given me a game ball. I'll never forget what Coach said. He turned to them and said "Little Joe is just playing the way we expect him to play. Now, when he does something beyond what we expect of him, he'll get a ball!"

Well, that statement meant more to me than receiving the actual game ball, and it remains one of the highest compliments I received throughout my career. You see, I knew right then what Coach Switzer really thought of me. With that one statement, Coach said more to me than if he had given me a ball, because what others (my teammates) saw as above average, he saw as my norm. So instead of being given the game ball, I was given a whole lot of pressure and expectations to live up to going forward! But I didn't mind; I met the challenge every day because I never wanted to disappoint Coach. So, did I worry about whether or not I got the credit? No, I never played the game with that in mind. If I had, I would have been playing for all of the wrong reasons.

The team was a special brotherhood, and we formed bonds that are strong to this day. We were a group of guys that understood that if we were going to be successful, we needed everyone else to do their part and BE a part. And, as we aged, we realized even more that we are still special to one another and really do need each other. Dave Robertson, our cool, long-haired quarterback from 1972 brought this to my attention while he was back in Norman for an Oklahoma game. He is the same cool guy today, just older cool.

There is no way I could look into a mirror and utter the words, "Well, Joe, you did it." I'd have a thousand friends and relatives slapping me upside my head. One group of guys that deserve credit is our group of "big guys," the offensive linemen that blocked their hearts out for me over the years.

The word "consistently" is what separates the real goods from the ordinaries. Sometimes they are nameless, but a football team lives or dies on the level of the offensive line's strength and tenacity. These are the guys who get the least amount of notoriety, and they could never be given too much credit.

Believe it or not, I always wished I could have been a lineman. I have always had the greatest respect for those big guys, especially the center, the first guy to break the huddle. Real men, gentle giants, the closest thing a guy can experience in what it's like to have a bodyguard. I loved the guys who opened the way for me, blocked for me, never seeking credit—they just did their job. If the back was successful then the lineman was successful.

During my freshman year, the offensive line, coached by Billy Michaels, was Dean Unruh, Tom Brahaney, Ken Jones, Eddie Foster and John Roush. My sophomore year, the starters were Eddie Foster, Terry Webb, center Kyle Davis, John Roush and Jerry Arnold. My junior year, we had Roush, Davis, Arnold, Webb, Jamie Melendez, Jim Taylor, Mike Vaughan and Drake Andarakes. My senior year, we added Chez Evans, Karl Baldischwiler, and the late Dennis Buchanan, who was the poster boy for not caring who got the credit. But this was the nature of our linemen and a major reason why we won consistently. These guys took great pride in throwing blocks that enable the running backs to score touchdowns. I don't know if you've noticed but when a running back scores, the big linemen are in the end zone celebrating with the running backs. The reason I bring this up is in some cases the running back has scored from 40 or more yards out and these big guys have blocked at the line of scrimmage (allowing the running back to score) and then sprinted the same distance as the running back to the end zone to participate in the celebration.

I have to give credit also to a family whose influence, class and involvement set the standard of what Sooners strive to be. Their involvement has been paramount to the status and success of the University of Oklahoma. There is no way possible to talk about anything pertaining to Oklahoma that is good and not mention the Selmons. You are talking about an outstanding group of players and people. The Selmon brothers and family are such an important part of Oklahoma and OU football.

My Coach

Coach Barry Switzer will forever be revered in my memory. My brother created the silver shoes, but Coach allowed them to fly. I have nightmares thinking about where I would be if he had not been my coach. He loved the game, but he loved his players more. He taught us all to not worry about who gets the credit, and he didn't do this in any speech—he lived it. There was never a time I felt he didn't have my best interest at heart. I may not have agreed with his opinion at every moment, but as a coach's son, I always understood.

There were a couple times I can remember getting a little weirder than I usually was, and he may have felt it was a reflection on him. It wasn't you, Coach, it was me dealing with my personal demons and expectations. I was lucky to be at the university at this time. Coach was exactly who I needed him to be as I found my place at OU. The man is a living legend, a national treasure to us all, but for me, he was a caring person I learned a lot from, and not necessarily through conversations, but from just being in his presence. Out of the thousands of football players he has coached, all of us, still to this day seek his acknowledgment and approval. He'll forever be *my coach*.

I have to mention also Port G. Robertson, one of the assistant athletic directors at OU in charge of everything. No athlete during Port's tenure has come through here and not been touched or influenced by him in some positive way. If nothing else, there are 1,240 Port stories floating around. What's kind of funny, though, is I have returned to a position at the university at the same age as the revered man was at the time I was an athlete. That translates into a careful perspective I am constantly aware of. His age doesn't appear to be as old now. So now I'm the one, the elder statesman, and Father Time has never missed a tackle.

You can see some of yourself in the young athletes coming through our sports programs at the university. They are highly recruited and had fantastic high school careers. I know what their questions will be once they hit the campus, because I asked them too: "Will I be able to live up to everyone's expectations? Will I be able to live up to my expectations?" They are just kids who are now exposed to the pressures of major college football.

They create an unbelievable source of revenue for the university, especially when they are successful. Yes, they are playing football in exchange for an education, but, I truly feel there is still a bit of inequity in this deal. These young people are not just student-athletes. Why? Another kid on any other scholarship has one task–keeping their grades up. The athlete on scholarship, however, has additional pressures. He, or she, is expected to make good grades, while their performance in sports is publicly scrutinized. They must also dedicate hours of practice honing their craft. Performance is mandatory in order to keep their scholarship. Only athletes know the weight of the burden and the pressure to perform each and every day.

The college athlete actually has two sets of parents; home and at school, which means he is still getting screamed at, which ain't all bad. I just think these kids (and they are kids) deserve more credit than what they receive for what they do and endure.

I try to think of what I needed to hear when I was their age, and maybe it will give them one more day of perspective until they get that next breath of inspiration. If I had to boil it down to some general words of advice they would be: remember the people who made your success possible, every member of a team is important, work hard to get better every day, be a part of the team, and don't worry about who gets the credit.

By allowing us to hang around him every day, our dad laid the foundation, guiding me and Kim down the path to being two of the most confident and fearless people on earth. Dad never told us many things, if at all, about having confidence, but he made us believe everything is possible when you work hard. And the harder you work, the more opportunities come your way.

In conjunction with being the athletic director and football coach, Dad also coached track for the high school. While the track team was working out, Kim and I spent our time jumping the hurdles. We weren't real good. Kim was only in the 1st grade and it was a little difficult for him to jump the regular hurdles. I was in 3rd grade and I could jump them, but without the greatest of form.

In those days the hurdles were made of heavy wood and one day Dad took a couple of those hurdles to the wood-working shop at his school and had them cut down so the height of the hurdles were relative to our size. At the time, I didn't even know he was aware of our interest in the hurdles. I mentioned earlier that my folks never forced us into doing anything, but if we showed an interest and wanted to do something, they did everything to accommodate us. So at our young ages my dad taught us how to hurdle and we became skilled little hurdlers with perfect form. By teaching us to hurdle, Dad gave me a skill that would become one of my signature moves.

Referring back to our chapter, most detrimental to any team are the overt displays of extreme selfishness on the part of some members. This is also true, not only in athletics, but within corporations, philanthropic organizations, or churches, etc. But, let's take football for instance. A selfish act may not be directly related to the sport. It may be a decision to break curfew, attracting negative publicity in some manner, or getting into a fight when the player could have just walked away. By the way, there are a lot of consequences and outcomes when a fight takes place. When you avoid a fight you might get called a 'wus' and your pride will hurt a little, but, just remember, he who runs away–lives to fight another day.

We live in a society today where most don't hesitate to take the credit or bring attention to themselves for every little thing, even for doing a job they are expected to do. How about those athletes that feel they deserve special recognition for everything, all the time? They want the exclusive credit for an entire season, a special win, a championship, or an individual play. They are over the top when they get credit for sacking the QB one time, but what are they doing the other 40 plays? Granted, its tough to make a good play every time and there may be a special circumstance or situation where you celebrate, not just because you feel you deserve it, but because it is a natural reaction to the team's success. I am so grateful to my folks that at an early age I was able to understand that one person does not a team make. In other words, do not be a prima donna, act like you've been in the end zone before.

I much prefer seeing a player make a great play, then acting as if it is just the norm. And, I can always appreciate a player who understands that he is just one part of the whole package. It would be pretty tough to line up with eight men going against 11, it takes everyone. Better yet, envision me carrying the ball with no blocking. My dad and great coaches have always pounded away with that one message: it takes a *team* to play, to succeed, or achieve. But you would be surprised to learn even some coaches think *they* should get the most credit, that they are the most important factor.

One great coach with whom I am quite familiar, Coach Switzer, once said, "Players win games, coaches lose them." No one member of a team can or should take total credit, or be given total credit, ever. There is no success without someone else contributing. No matter what it is or how great it is.

Now, there are some people in the workplace that are so concerned with who gets the credit, they ignore the team's achievements, or de-emphasize the contributions of others in order to relish in their own moment of glory. Unselfish employees know they have risen to the top because many people contributed to their success. In most instances they get to that point because their colleagues and supervisors are *true* team players. We should never fail to credit the people in the background, on the sidelines, at home, or in the stands. Let's not forget to give credit where it is due. We all stood on someone's shoulders to get where we are.

Yes, praise and credit are important to not only receive, but also to give because being the recipient of praise and/or credit is part of what confirms our efforts and helps us continue to believe in ourselves, believe in what we are doing, and builds the confidence needed to keep us moving forward. Giving praise is equally as important as receiving it because it creates a balanced society. Individuals who have reached a certain level of success are especially in a good position to give praise because there will be individuals striving to reach greater levels who need to hear encouraging words coming from someone who holds the position for which they are striving. When you receive praise from someone at the top you know you are doing something right and you will feel the appreciation and incentive that will push you to keep trying. I try to take every opportunity to offer words of praise or give credit to a youngster playing football because I remember how much it lifted me when a player from my team complimented me.

Again, it balances out our society. At some point you will be the one striving to "make it to the top" and in need of praise and credit. Then, once you're there, it will be your turn to give back to those in the position you once were in.

Now, that's not to say that one should chase praise. Strategizing and positioning yourself in order to receive praise will more than likely leave you disappointed, unfulfilled and rather annoying to those around you. Have you ever worked with someone who would do anything to get the boss's attention and approval? Talk about irritating. Most of all, if you solicit praise you will never feel the true power of receiving an unadulterated compliment because your actions will be all for the wrong reasons. Others may not realize this but deep down, you know. In a team situation, the minute you start focusing on personally getting the praise is the minute you stop focusing on the team.

When you do receive a compliment, take the time to really appreciate the words that were said to you. Recognize that a compliment is generally expressed when you have met or exceeded someone's personal standards, so they are not only expressing their approval of you, but also expressing their respect for you. A compliment is somewhat of an intangible gift we carry with us.

Along with encouraging student athletes to do their best to further the tradition here at Oklahoma, I also feel that it is appropriate for them to understand unequivocally the responsibilities they inherit and to appreciate the fact that they are part of a group. Acting as if you are *not* part of a group still affects the group. On more than one occasion I have stated, "It takes more than you to have success. No one person succeeds by himself." I hope it sinks in.

Individuals may want to take all the credit, but deep down it just has to register—if it weren't for a block, or the training program, a coach's encouragement, or another teammate doing their job, it wouldn't work. It takes everyone pulling their load. Like marriage, you have to be individually responsible, but understand that it takes two to tango.

I also feel that it's okay for teammates to be kind to each other and treat their team like their family, like the team is a special brotherhood or sisterhood. Support and encourage each in the same manner you'd want to be supported. Do it regardless. You might think it doesn't matter to them because:

1) Some players act as if they are too cool to want that support
2) They feel responding to or giving kindness shows they have feelings; perhaps a little soft spot that lessens their manhood–the greatest no-no.
3) Some athletes really believe there is no such thing as being a good, kind, respectable guy and then becoming a badass on the field. If you don't believe there is such a personae believe me, all I have to do is mention one name in the community of Oklahoma, we called him "Big Cat," Lee Roy Selmon. Big Cat, was one of the nicest guys on the planet and one of the baddest players on the football field. Lee Roy Selmon.

Try to truly care for each other, have each other's back, and always be a cheerleader for each other. The results will be deeply satisfying. You will be grateful, as I am, for friendships that have endured through the years.

I also often tell our students about those first few days when I arrived on campus at Oklahoma. I knew OU already had two Heisman winners in Billy Vessels and Steve Owens, plus many runners-up for the honor, and scores of All-Americans. I let the incoming kids know there's been a badass at their position before they got here and many will come after them. I know this to be true: I have witnessed it and lived it. Each athlete has a purpose, a window of opportunity here to make a difference. They need to make the most of their time at OU because it goes so fast. Don't end up being forty years old, just wishing you had done more on that fourth and one.

I believe you can have a smidgen of an attitude, an athletic arrogance if you will, because you are proud of your team; a team who strives to be the best. But a selfish attitude means you are too absorbed in your own performance to encourage others. On a team you are just a part, no matter how big the role, you're still just a part. Without the other components you are a big part of nothing.

The best team players don't fear another's success and will acknowledge it. In fact, they take delight in helping others achieve even greater things than they themselves accomplished.

I had a good appreciation of every coach I ever had, even the ones I wasn't tall enough to see eye-to-eye with. You see, I have a hard time not listening to everyone. I care what others think, and, like I've said before, I believe you can learn something from everyone, even people you dislike. You can even get something good from something bad; it may be a little tougher to find, but it's there. Life's lessons are never over, and I am still learning today. I thank God for those folks who cared enough to tell me the truth, to care for me when I may not have deserved their attention, who believed in me when I was struggling to believe in myself.

Take the time to thank someone who has made a difference in your life. It wouldn't hurt. They might have said something, done something that impacted you, and they never knew. It will be a blessing to them and you.

And then…

The room was quiet as I sat on a table getting ready to be taped up for my last high school football game. During spring training my high school had an annual game where the returning team would play against the graduating players. My dad had always taped my ankles before every game of my high school career; I see now it was our special tradition. I knew and he knew that this would probably be the final time he would tape me up. I was moving on to play for OU and would be taped by training staff from then on.

I will never forget how my dad came into the small training room. Without a word, he picked up the can of Tuff-skin, sprayed my ankles, picked up the tape, and began the process. Dad wound the tape around my ankles securely, lovingly, making sure there were no wrinkles in the tape. He was an expert at the procedure, and suddenly tears came to my eyes as I watched his hands doing what they had done for me so many times. I didn't even look to see if Dad was crying, too. Even if he wasn't, he had to have a lump in his throat, and I did see his normally steady hands quiver a bit. Both of us knew this moment would never be repeated.

He finished, got up, and walked slowly out of the room with his head down. I sat on the table a little longer. Neither one of us had spoken a word. To me it was a sacred moment frozen in time.

I couldn't possibly thank my father for countless hours on the football field, discipline in our home, and the unconditional love he offered to all of us. He was the most effective person in my life whether it was demonstrating in real life "how to" or "how not to." Thanks, Dad.

—Joe

SECRET #5

The Influence of Coaches Will Last a Lifetime

Before a football team begins their season's opening games there are a few weeks of practice where there are no real games, just practice games. College teams practice with the defense and offense going against their own team members. However, in high school, as well as in the pros, scrimmages are scheduled against other teams. Usually there are only simulated special teams for these scrimmages. There is action on the field, but no contact is allowed; no blocking or tackling; just positioning with the actual kicking or punting of the ball.

I recall a particular scrimmage when I was in the ninth grade. I was attending the high school where Dad coached and this was the first step of my lifelong dream; the dream of playing for my dad and with my brother, Kim. Kim was only in the seventh grade so he was still in junior high school at that time, but he was along for the trip as one of the "trainers".

Even though I was younger, I was hoping to play varsity as a freshman. Actually, I thought I was good enough to play varsity as a freshmen. But, I had no clue what my dad was thinking about that possibility. All I knew at this point was that I was going out to play with the junior varsity. That day we were scrimmaging with Aldine Carver High School from Houston, Texas. Since I was a little kid, Aldine and my dad's teams have scrimmaged each other. Sites were switched each year and this year we were in Houston. Usually, the varsity team started the scrimmage first, on one field, then later the junior varsity came in to get some playing time on another field. The junior varsity was never on the field as long as the varsity team.

So, the varsity started playing and I am sitting on the sideline with the junior varsity watching. After a while, I lose interest and start messing around with the other guys. The reason I have lost interest is because I am pissed; I think I should be out there with the varsity, which was not looking too good. I can tell Dad wasn't a happy camper. At this same moment I become aware that the horseplay is starting to get a little out of hand on the sidelines and that makes me nervous, so I start paying attention again to the scrimmage. Suddenly, one of the team managers came over to me and said, "Little Joe, your dad wants you."

I jogged onto the field where Dad was, knowing I was about to get chewed out for horsing around, but I was still steamed because I wasn't playing with the varsity. I stood next to him for what seemed like ten minutes and he didn't say a word. Finally I hear him ask without looking at me, "Do you think you can run against these guys?"

I answered without any hesitation, "Shoot yeah."
Immediately my heart is pumping and the hair on my neck is standing stiff. I am about to play with the varsity. All I can think about are all the times I had imagined myself carrying the football in this exact instance.
The only thing Dad said, was, "Alright, go back over there and sit down."
Now if you think I was pissed the first time, well now you can pan fry a steak well-done on my head. My temper subsided when the coaches told us to loosen up and stretch. I knew it was getting close to show time; our time to scrimmage. So, as I was jogging over to where we would scrimmage, that same manager pulled me aside and said again, "Little Joe, your dad wants you."
I am thinking now that he's lost his mind so I go over and Dad immediately asks, "Are you loose?"
"Yes."
"Okay, get in there."
For some reason I didn't hesitate, I went straight toward the varsity huddle like I belonged. However, as I ran to the huddle, it seemed like it was in slo-motion as my mind flashed back to that kid at 1208 Avenue B flying over the chairs and sofas. Will it be all that I had imagined? Will the ball feel the same? Am I what I imagined I would be? Will I take my place in the huddle and be part of that team? Will my legs shake? Will I get the chance to run flanker right split left 26? Will everything continue to be in slo-motion? The answer to all of those questions was a resounding, yes—it was just like I had imagined all those years. I loved the play "26"; it was perfect for me. It eventually became "26 Joe pick a hole," because it gave me the option to run wherever and however

I wanted. This was really happening and all the coaches for Aldine were raving and wanting to know who I was. Not until we were almost finished did they realize it was me "Little Joe", one of big Joe's two boys who had always been in the way carrying towels and acting like we belonged.

After the scrimmage was over I knew I had convinced everyone who had eyes that I could run with the football (especially the coaches of Aldine) and that I deserved to play on the varsity. We got on the bus to head back to Port Arthur. Dad says nothing about my performance except, "How do you feel?"

Verbally my answer was, "Okay, my back is a little sore," but, non-verbally I am saying "I am ready to play varsity. Didn't you see me, they couldn't touch me? What are you going to do. Are you going to move me up?"

The first game of the season came up the very next week and I fully expected to be in the starting line-up for the varsity team. But, I wasn't. Shucks, I wasn't even on the junior varsity team! I played on the freshman team for the first four games of the season, watching varsity from a distance like any other spectator.

Of course at the time, I didn't see that Dad was testing me. By keeping me on the freshman team he was measuring my desire to play, seeing if my abilities stood out first at the freshman level. All I saw was that he wasn't allowing me to play at the higher level where I knew I could contribute. However, this man was not just my dad, he was my coach and like it or not, I had to respect his decision in that role. And I would continue to respect the decisions of every coach I would have.

It isn't surprising that I would have the utmost respect for coaches. I have been around them in some capacity all of my life. I am the son of a coach, a player and a huge supporter. Only coaches themselves and the players they have impacted, know what they are really about.

So, let's talk about a coach's power, or just the power of power; some respect it and some abuse it. We've heard heroic stories of individuals in power and we've heard horror stories of individuals in power. The stories have consisted of individuals from all ranks of life: politicians, teachers, clergymen, CEO's, servicemen, etc.

One of the most influential and powerful groups of professionals who fit this power category are coaches. Being a coach's son I have had the advantage of seeing and being around some very good ones and some not so good ones. These guys are a very unique and rare breed, and in most cases a weird breed, and this would include my dad who coached more than forty years. As a kid growing up and even into my early professional years it was nearly impossible for me to question a coach's decisions no matter how far off base I thought he was.

Before we were even old enough to play football, my younger brother Kim and I hung out a lot in a room we called the 'cage'. It was the room with all the football equipment for the highschool team. The back wall was concrete cinder block with some windows, but they were barred. The front wall looked like one big animal cage with a sliding door. There was a cutout window so you wouldn't have to always open the big sliding door every time a guy on the team came up to get something. We were always back there going through all the equipment, plus handing out equipment; shoes, pants, helmets, shoulder pads and even jock straps. We examined every item in order to see if there was anything that would fit us. We often even discovered designs by the sports manufacturer that we could improve on.

In my day, only a few kids got to wear the full gear of the authentic football player. This was because you didn't start playing organized football until Junior High School. When you first came out for football and were given your equipment, the coach gave you the instructions on how to put this equipment on properly. You were given a helmet, chinstrap, shoulder pads, in some cases rib pads, hip pads, a web belt with a double round buckle, (sometimes the coach had to go over this part three times because the buckle was tricky), pants with two separate thigh pads, two separate knee pads, socks, jockstraps and shoes.

Well, of course, Kim and I knew all of that stuff about the equipment because we had heard Dad instruct players a hundred times. We could repeat the instructions as well as he did. Every opportunity that presented itself we would dress out in full gear head to toe, shoes, socks and even jocks. Then, we'd take all the gear off and do it all over again, sometimes repeating what the coaches instructions were, especially about the knee pads, because at that time, the way they made the pockets for the kneepads could be a little challenging–but not for us.

Putting on that uniform became a ritual that was carefully choreographed by every football player from pee wees to the ultimate pro and you can be assured, that in most cases, the progression was pretty much the same each time.

When very young, the first thing I associated with a coach was that coaches carried whistles; a sign that they were in charge. Maybe it's the whistle that can somehow turn an ordinary Joe into a coach who is a positive influencing factor in a kid's life, or a coach that leaves a lot to be desired. Of course, most coaches screamed a lot, but the one thing that overshadowed all was how the good ones were always telling or showing someone, something. Coaches are so important, especially a kid's first coach. Hopefully that first coach will not have a negative impact on any child. Parents should ask about a coach's motivation for coaching your child. Is he all about winning or is his goal to build a sound and healthy sports foundation for the kid? A coach's impact can be a life altering experience that potentially shapes a kids views and societal outlook.

There are numerous levels of coaching, the first level being, as stated already, probably the most important; the coach for a kid just entering organized sports. Let's say, for instance, that sport is football. The kid will experience putting on equipment for the first time, as explained above, and he will be participating in perhaps the toughest sport there is, especially during practice. Football is based on contact, contact, and more contact so with all of these tangibles involved, including the fact that six year olds are now introduced to the sport, I would say having a good coach who can communicate with young players is extremely important.

But, really, what is this coach going to do most of the time with six year olds? Well, other than tying a lot of shoestrings, and buttoning up more chin straps than Carter has pills everyday, he mostly will be picking up the kids when they fall because the oversized equipment is so cumbersome. A kid's first time coach has got to be encouraging, positive and kind but also tough enough to convince a six year old that it is perfectly okay to stick that helmet he's wearing into that stiff tackling dummy. Or, he deals with the bully of a kid who outweighs most of the others by 25 pounds and just pushes smaller kids down just because he can. The coach of these smallest of athletes should be occupied with giving more high fives and pats on the butt than the number of times he takes a breath in a day. I'm sure for most coaches at this level, investing in these children is one of the most rewarding things they can do. The coach who first instills a love of sports in kids will experience tranquil and satisfying times.

What should a kid get out of this introductory phase to sports (football in particular)?

- He should know how to put on the necessary equipment and why each item is important to the sport.
- He should also learn the fundamentals of every position, including the basic stances like the two point, three point, and four point stance.
- Coach has to make sure little Johnny is looking through his facemask and not under his facemask and helmet. I promise you it is necessary.

- The child should also be told again and again how each member of the team is important and how each one must play their part to have a successful team.

Of course, a kid should first learn the fundamentals of any sport. I don't think you immediately become good at playing until you learn the fundamentals and do the little things well. Having speed and size can disguise the lack of fundamentals for just so long, then sooner or later this deficiency will raise its head.

Parents ask me often about their kids playing sports. "When should they start?" "Should Johnny concentrate on only one sport," etc. I advocate that kids participating in sports and other extracurricular activities shouldn't have to choose between any sport. Baseball, soccer, or even basketball should maybe be among the first sports they try, or even swimming. Football too, as long as it's flag. Let them participate in what they like to do, if that is one thing or several things. Or, they may want to try a musical instrument. Participation in any sport, or extracurricular activity, should place a child into a positive environment where the end result is beneficial to not only their physical development but their character development as well.

I can hear it now, "But, Joe, my kid is on a team that never wins. How can that be good for him/her?" Well, it is a fact, that in order to win, a team must have some good players. If not, they will most likely lose to the better players on the opposing team. However, the smart, insightful coach will find things to celebrate even in a loss. To point out small victories, like players' improvement or their great effort goes a long way in encouraging kids. It is how the coach handles the losses, or the wins for that matter, that will impact the kids going forward.

There are other basic areas that coaches at this level must communicate with these young athletes and their parents:

1) There is no bullying allowed whether on the field, at school, or any where.
2) We expect you to do the right thing.
3) If you happen to be a good player, it means as a good player, we expect you to work harder and we expect more from you.
4) If you are not a great player (or starter) we still expect you to work harder and get better. If you work hard and hustle it will be noticed and effort will be rewarded.
5) You will learn the fundamentals of every position.
6) You will learn how to work together and you will learn and understand that team means everybody.
7) The coach should make time to meet with the parents to gain insight as to what the parents expect. Both parents and coaches may have hidden agendas. Most parents start off okay and say all the right things, but the truth will set them free. In reality, all they really want is for little Johnnie to be the star quarterback.

This may seem overstated, but I feel the coach has to be that person outside the family to express these points and enforce them with passion and kindness. Two other points that I need to make is that, one, some coaches, in wanting to win at all costs, try to make the game much too complicated for these youngsters. In my opinion, there needs to be a written criteria that limits the number of plays that can be used in Little League football. It is the parents' responsibility to monitor the true intentions of these appointed coaches who make the game much too advanced for little bodies and minds.

Then, too, there is the coach who has a child of his own on the team he or she coaches. In most cases, no matter how he tries, he isn't objective where his kid is concerned. This coach may place his or her child in a starting position when he is not prepared nor is he the best player suited for that spot, or, he goes the other way, refusing to give his child a starting position because of how it will look to others; even though his child is clearly a starter. Parents have to make sure the coaches at this level give every young participant a balance of consideration, compassion, discipline, and encouragement. Remember these kids are only first, second, or third graders, not contenders for a Super Bowl ring.

There probably aren't too many other situations where favoritism is more obvious than in organized sports. The skilled players are the ones who play; everyone else doesn't. Naturally, the "starters" are kids with the best skills. In little leagues, all of the kids play no matter how talented they are. However, as the child gets older and winning becomes more important, somehow the "every child gets an opportunity to play" mentality is dropped as competitive lines are drawn. The kids who are good enough to play become the ones that everyone congratulates after a win or consoles after a loss; they become the ones whose names are yelled out across the field by the encouraging fans. Kids on the side lines, just waiting for the opportunity to play, often feel left out or overlooked. Obviously, all children cannot be starters but that doesn't mean they should be pushed to the side or receive less attention.

At this formative level, a coach should understand he is not Bill Belichick coaching the New England Patriots. He should still be coaching every player on the team and communicating what each kid needs to work on for improvement. Every child at this level needs encouragement.

The magnitude of the affect that a coach has on a child is comparable to that of a parent to a child and should be taken that seriously? It only takes one coach to make a negative remark and you can watch the most confident child question his or her abilities. Suddenly mom and dad's opinion no longer carries the same weight; they want the approval from the coach. At some point, a child decides that mom and dad are only praising him because he is their child.

Sure, coaches are going to discover the players that have great potential. But finding a player with special talent is almost as bad as the coach thinking that he is the greatest coach on the planet. Some coaches compromise themselves and the entire team by thinking a gifted athlete may be their personal step to stardom. It happens all the time. The coach begins to favor the gifted athlete, then the athlete senses that he's getting treated a little differently by the coach. He sees that his effort at practice can be a little less enthusiastic, or he can even miss practice, or bend the rules and get away with it. A good coach can appreciate the skills of a great athlete but must communicate that it is that athlete's unselfish attitude and dedicated approach to being part of a team that really makes him a great or special player.

I think this tendency for a coach to ride the coattails of a great player is intensified at the high school level. Think about it. A guy starts coaching at a high school and his livelihood most of the time depends on the performance of teenagers – then he finds a special player who has the ability to change a program and make the coach look good as well. The wise coach knows he has to focus and invest in every young person's life, not just the most talented ones. I've always thought the best coaches paid attention and gave attention, too. And they communicated. The best communicated and they allowed the athlete to communicate. When this road was a one way street results weren't positive.

Here's a perfect example: I knew a high school soccer player who had a bi-lateral hip flexor tear at the end of her freshman year. The doctor told her she had to rest or she could cause permanent damage to herself. She rested several weeks during summer, but the varsity coach had given a strict set of daily workouts that each player was to be prepared to complete in order to try out for varsity and she knew that the coach thought any injuries (other than a broken bone) were a direct result of improper conditioning. Try outs came and she refused to tell him about her injury because she knew he would think she hadn't stuck to his summer regimen. She also feared he would see her injury as a risk and cut her from the team. Throughout tryouts, she was in pain but never said one word. When she ran timed laps with the group, she fell to the back one-third when she normally would have been leading the pack. The coach yelled at her for falling behind, but still she refused to tell him the truth as to why. And there was one more rule: Parents were not allowed to intervene and/or call the coach.

If a child is afraid to give their coach a note from a doctor because he or she may not make the team, or if said coach does not communicate with parents, one has to wonder about the degree of power we are allowing coaches to have. Such behavior could result in permanent physical injury to a child. Remember, we are talking about kids, not paid professionals. So, the young lady made the team, recovered from her injury and proved herself to the coach. But it came with a price; it changed her as a person.

Coaching is a position often misunderstood and greatly under-appreciated. The number one occupational hazard for coaches is frustration usually because a coach knows what should be done and it isn't happening. That can be frustrating. A coach and his staff can prepare for a game, create a game plan, but as soon as the whistle blows to start the game or even a play, any control he had leaves his hands. The coach becomes just another spectator because he can't perform the actions required. No matter how ingenious the game plan, the coach has to leave the implementation of the plan up to his players. He can only depend on the actions of youngsters who can barely be where they are to be without someone herding them. He is unable to even step on the field during a game by threat of penalty. The coach can't throw a pass, catch a pass, kick a field goal, or line up on the defensive line. When things aren't going right, I can just imagine a coach's frustration at this lack of control. His only hope is that players do what they have been taught to do.

During my high school playing days, and even still today, a football coach might also be a basketball, wrestling, or baseball coach as well. The head basketball coach for our high school was Coach James Gamble, but he also coached the receivers and defensive backs for our football team. Dick Williams was responsible for the defensive line, but he was also the baseball coach. Carl Jackson was quarterback coach and track coach who had actually played quarterback for Dad years before. He ran track and was a 25 foot long jumper in college and one of my early sports idols. There was also Leroy Leopold who coached track and the offensive line. Coach Leopold's son, Bobby, played for my dad after I graduated then he went on to play in the pros. Coach Ellis Wise, Coach Johnny Hamilton and Coach Cordell Lindsay handled the freshmen and Coach Wayne Williams was coach for the linebackers. What great impressions each one of them made in my life.

A coach teaches players the fundamentals of the game which often can be related to different phases of life. A coach trains players in the correct way to play the game, he shows them strategies and techniques to develop and strengthen their skills. He has a game plan to take the team to victory when put into play, and hopefully has the appropriate words to help them accept and understand a loss when it happens. Since my father was both dad and coach, I never really differentiated between the roles, because Dad coached me as a father my entire life. I didn't realize how all of the techniques and skills that he taught me as a child would be what made me so unique as a player.

Again, it is very true that a coach's actions or opinions may have a profound effect on youngsters. A gifted coach knows that each child may respond differently to coaching and they may need different methods of motivation. When you look at the dynamics of coaches and players it is easy to see how a parental role may be established with a child. The coach provides direction, praise, discipline, authority, and the child reacts accordingly. Sadly, in some cases, a coach is the only real model of a parent, especially a dad, that some children have. This is also why a bad coach can discourage, demoralize, and break a child's spirit.

That being said, a coach's personality has a great deal to do with his coaching style. A coach's message doesn't always have to be delivered with a ton of bricks; the drill sergeant approach to coaching. Some of the greatest coaches have been quiet men, soft-spoken but effective on and off the field. Bud Wilkinson, the long time coach of Oklahoma during the teams' glory days of the '50's, rarely raised his voice. His easy going speech and methodical game plans proved to be successful for over 17 years. Then there's Ohio State's Woody Hayes, Alabama's 'Bear' Bryant, or basketball coach, Bobby Knight, known for their emotional outbursts and "in your face" style of coaching. Yet, these coaches were effective, successful and deeply-loved by their players.

It depends on the player, but discipline or instruction handed down in even tones can be as effective for some as the screaming and yelling most often associated with a coach's demeanor. But if that kid understands the coach's tirade is nothing personal and he expects more of himself than any coach ever could, that approach falls off his back like water off a duck. However, can you imagine the fallout from employees or the public if a CEO or political leader spoke to his employees or constituents in this manner? Yet, it is often acceptable behavior from football coaches, perhaps because football is a tough and violent sport. And, as stated, coaching is not an easy vocation; if it were, everyone would want to do it.

Again, I learned from every coach and I know this is going to sound a bit strange, but I had most trouble relating to taller, bigger coaches over 6' 3". Plain and simple we just didn't see eye to eye!

Many people picture coaches as stodgy, straight-laced, boring people with no sense of humor; never seen smiling on the sidelines. However, coaches can be fun-loving men who enjoy being in the company of players and fellow coaches. Some of my most memorable times were spent seeing my dad with his coaching staff. They would sit around, laugh, play checkers and have fun with each other even while grading players, looking at film, or putting together a game plan.

Even as a youngster I realized that these fun-loving coaches had a low tolerance for bullies who made life miserable for smaller, weaker kids. When participating in sports, most children discover early that there is a pecking order as to who is in charge in every group. You learn who the mean kids are, who was going to be a competitor, or who would be a quitter, a whiner. Even simple games like marbles, baseball, even 'hiding the switch', were often contests of personalities. My upbringing taught me that trying to take advantage of someone's weakness, especially if they were friends was not a good idea unless it was a sports competition. Teasing or making fun of someone who couldn't do everything well was not tolerated.

When I was in the sixth grade I joined in when other kids began razzing a little, defenseless girl. Later, I was guilt-ridden; devastated that I had been a part of hurting her emotionally and never did that again. I was beginning to understand I didn't have to go along with the crowd to prove myself in any way. Years later I called her to apologize but I don't think she remembered the incident, which was good.

Even rookies in the pros are not exempt from razzing. Traditionally, rookies are singled out, often during team dinners, constantly being called upon to sing their school song amidst all kinds of harassment. When my time came, it was no big deal – I just kept singing even when they tried to boo me off stage. I learned to sing even louder and worse until they eventually stopped calling on me to sing. Sure, it was funny at times, but I determined as a veteran player that I would not be a part of harassing the rookies. I mean a wild-eyed rookie has enough on his mind trying to make the team, much less worrying about auditioning to be Tom Jones.

I told a story in the introduction of this chapter about my first experience playing for my dad as a freshman. The conclusion of that first real experience with my dad as a coach was epic. Remember, I had just proven what I could do with a football under my arm and I had done well, and it wasn't enough. I couldn't understand why my coach would leave me on that freshman team. The frustration behind the questions to which I couldn't find answers was a whole new ball game to me. My point here is to point out the power a coach has over a player. He knew what his intentions were for me as a player, but I had no idea what those intentions were, so there was a lack of communication and the ripple effect was huge. He probably didn't give it a second thought, but that was all I could think about. For the very first time my dad and my coach were no longer one in the same. Right then and there, he was singularly just my coach. I never forgot that feeling.

I didn't tie the fact that this is a normal feeling between most kids and their coaches until I grew up and watched the affects coaches had on my own daughter. Watching how a coach impacted her confidence, both good and bad, is when it all hit me full force. That is when I could see the true power of a coach. Under the good ones, she flourished; under the bad ones, not so. How could the confident girl we knew from years of building her up, suddenly be so negatively impacted by the comments from one person; an outsider in our lives?

All too often, by the time it is realized that a specific coach isn't a good fit for a child; the damage has already been done. So, with coaches, we have the good and bad just like everything else. Whether you are parent of a child or a coach of a group of children, the power of a coach can never be discounted or taken lightly. The impact a coach makes upon a child may be life long and coaches should be both praised and appreciated as well as held accountable when it applies.

I can't leave this section about coaches that influenced me without mentioning one of my favorite coaches and individuals: Coach Wendell Mosley. Coach is a legend not only because of coaching some of the greatest backs in the country but also because of his unique personality, his incomparable sense of humor, and his drive to be big time.

One day in the late '80's, I received a call from Greg Pruitt. He said, "Little Joe, if you want to see Coach – better go see him now. He doesn't have much time left." Coach Mosley had been diagnosed with cancer and was in the Veterans Hospital in Dallas and no one expected him to return home. These would be his last days. Mike (Mad Dog) Phillips from Galveston, Texas picked me up at the Dallas airport and drove me over to see Coach Mosley. We had been recruited from Texas together. We found the hospital and Mad Dog dropped me off and I went looking for Coach – walking the halls, sticking my head in and out of hospital rooms. Some were empty, others occupied. Then, I peeked in one room, and I observed Coach in his pajamas, hair all over the place. I make note of this because I never saw Coach with a hair out of place in his whole life. He was lying on his left side, curled in a fetal position writhing in bed, obviously in great pain. You could see it even if your eyes were closed, because his sounds of pain were very clear and even though he was in very bad shape, I knew it was Coach. I was shocked at the sight of his physical being. He had always been the picture of perfect health. I backed out of the room before he saw me, withdrawing back into the hall taking deep breaths trying to decide what to do and how to go back into his room. As if on cue and answering my question a nurse called out, "Can I help you?"

In a raised voice (so that Coach could hear me), I answered, "Yes, I am looking for Coach Wendell Mosley."

She replied, " You mean, Frazier?"

I said, "Yes."

She said, "Well, you are right there – his room is right there," and she motioned to the door. I was hoping that Coach heard me and would recognize my voice.

I entered the room again and this time, Coach had transformed himself into my backfield coach, the man who had recruited me and bragged about me to the OU coaches. So much so, that they had laughed and accused him of being on drugs. With eyes, now bright and alert, he said, "Hey, big boy…how you doing?"

He was sitting up, one hand resting behind his head, clothing straightened, hair brushed back, composed with that big grin. He was his dignified self, grateful for the visit, wanting to hear about me. I would never forget the experience. Coach Mosley was a proud man with a boat load of pride and dignity and I could see it on his face that he was excited to see me and have me visit, but I knew he was in a lot of pain. I also knew he was still in total control of his mind and body, he had just pulled himself together to see me. Everything about him and his words seemed the same, his emotions, and his demeanor even while suffering through the last stages of cancer were evidence of the coach I knew. I wanted to stay longer but for obvious reasons I knew it was time for me to go. This final experience with Coach Mosley made me appreciate him even more as a coach and human being. Coach, even on his dying bed, demonstrated to me as he did so many times before why I loved and had so much respect for him; a great influence in my life. He passed away a couple of days after that visit. I still miss him and I think of the man every day.

The coaches and people I most admired even as a youngster always tried to do the right thing. I hope people remember me in that same way. In fact, that became my definition of integrity – doing what is right.

***

And then…

I remember everything about my dad as a dad and as a coach. The most visible personalities in my life were my father and my coach which were of course one and the same. "The man" wore every hat imaginable, disciplinarian, teacher, trainer, conditioning coach and physical therapist.

I knew what he expected of his players by watching him through out the years, and I knew the whys and wherefores of every play in his playbook. My brother and I hung on his every word and wanted to be just like him. And when I played for him, he was already aware of my capabilities, my strengths and my weaknesses. I didn't have a coach for only two hours a day, or three times a week during the football season. I had a coach 24 hours a day, 365 days a year for my entire life. I never knew the advantage I had over others because of this until adulthood. How lucky I was that my dad knew most everything about me, and if I missed a cut or two, he knew there was usually a good reason. All during those critical, confidence building years of adolescence sports, I always had my dad and the coaches on his staff. It helped build me through that comfortable environment. I carried his teachings in my actions throughout my football career, these were born and developed by being in his environment and by observing everything that took place in his teachings with his players and coaches. But, what was key was my ability to instantly enact or put into play all I had been taught. Even when Dad wasn't coaching me, I was still privy to coaching through watching him at his practices or just listening to him talk to the other coaches. I did not have to prove my athletic ability to my father, but I did have to prove how far I was willing to go with it. Let's face it, when your son is a 168 pound back going up against players nearly twice his size, it would be difficult not to question his safety.

My first year in the pros was the last year the college All Stars played against the Super Bowl champions. That final year the Super Bowl champs were the Pittsburgh Steelers and the annual game was held in Chicago at Soldier Field. Well, to make a long story short, I handled my little self quite well, made good precise moves, kept away from that solid hit from the Steelers and managed to protect myself by not allowing one of their tacklers to hold me up while the rest of their teammates could finish me off. By surviving that game and being voted the MVP, my dad for the first time ever, realized that I could handle my 168 pound self. It probably enabled him to watch my games without freaking out. But even at this point in my life of playing professional football, he still offered his coaching points to me each week before each game. And I listened and respected his advice and appreciated his interest. I have got to thank my mom, too, who actually coached my Dad in the background by stepping in when she saw fit and leveling *out the bumpy roads a coach and his sons would surely encounter. Thanks, Mom and Dad for being the best team of coaches a kid could have and also for showing me how to be a man of integrity. Sadly, we would lose our mom on November 23, 1997.*

I have known from an early age that coaches must possess a ton of different qualities to be successful and occasionally that doesn't mean winning a championship 100 percent of the time. The words of the time honored poem, IF by Rudyard Kipling, I include here because it says it all. It not only states the attributes coaches should have, but what we all should strive as individuals to be.

IF

If you can keep your head when all about you
Are losing theirs and blaming it on you,
If you can trust yourself when all men doubt you,
But make allowance for their doubting too;
If you can wait and not be tired by waiting,
Or being lied about, don't deal in lies,
Or being hated, don't give way to hating,
And yet don't look too good, nor talk too wise:

If you can dream—and not make dreams your master,
If you can think—and not make thoughts your aim;
If you can meet with Triumph and Disaster
And treat those two impostors just the same;
If you can bear to hear the truth you've spoken
Twisted by knaves to make a trap for fools,
Or watch the things you gave your life to, broken,
And stoop and build 'em up with worn-out tools:

If you can make one heap of all your winnings
And risk it all on one turn of pitch-and-toss,

And lose, and start again at your beginnings
And never breath a word about your loss;
If you can force your heart and nerve and sinew
To serve your turn long after they are gone,
And so hold on when there is nothing in you
Except the Will which says to them: "Hold on!"

If you can talk with crowds and keep your virtue,
Or walk with kings—nor lose the common touch,
If neither foes nor loving friends can hurt you,
If all men count with you, but none too much;
If you can fill the unforgiving minute
With sixty seconds' worth of distance run,
Yours is the Earth and everything that's in it,
And—which is more—you'll be a Man, my son!

     Rudyard Kipling (1865-1936)

I can't add much to those great words, but I know men and women have touched my life and added clarity, direction, and inspiration. Here are some final thoughts that come to me as I remember those people.

They did right, because it was just right, without flinching in the wake of the consequences. They were that same conscientious human beings all the time. Their success may have been attributed to other factors, but they were respected mostly because they had integrity. For them, it was the end result of discipline, focus, faith, and goodness.

They couldn't fake integrity – it came out in the way they lived.

—Joe

Not a clear picture of us, but a real picture of us. Mom is behind the camera. Now, she and Pat have both passed on.

Pat and me in front of our 1950 Power Glide Chevrolet. Notice the stance. I was poised to make a cut.

Me and Dad on back campus of his first school – Hilliard High – 1960. I kept my wallet in the cuff of my pants.

Mom in glasses with baseball cap on backwards. She was with her students on field trip to Corpus Christi, Texas, in 1960. That's Kim in background hanging out of the door of the '57 Chevrolet.

Brother Kim, #19, handing ball off to me, #24, in high school. We were playing cross-town rivals, Thomas Jefferson. Together, we were unbeatable!

Scoring on play above. Hurdled #44 from at least four yards out—not a very good landing in end zone.

Getting a lot of attention after scoring my last touchdown in High School. Coach Williams and Coach Leopold putting me on stretcher after breaking my leg. The last game of my high school career.

Following my injury, Kim conferring and planning strategy with coaches Wayne Williams, Carl Jackson, Leroy Leopold, and Richard Williams.

Freshman year OU press photo, 1972.

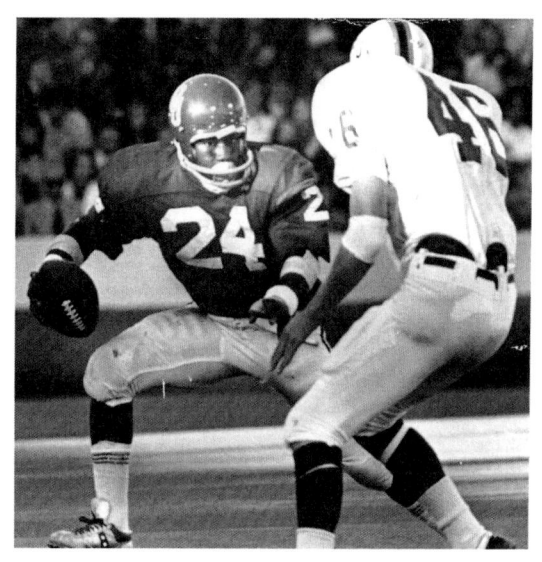

Freshman game vs. OSU, defender is looking at how the ball is being carried, not at me.

Same game, same play, different angle and in color. Signature grip—if I need to throw the ball, I can do it without changing the grip. I always joked that whenever I fumbled, I was holding the football the conventional way.

Sports Illustrated cover 1974 against Wake Forest. Jim Littrell in foreground. They didn't acknowledge Jim and me by giving our names on cover due to probation that year.

Probably the most familiar picture of me in an OU uniform vs. Utah State my sophomore year. #23 didn't make the tackle.

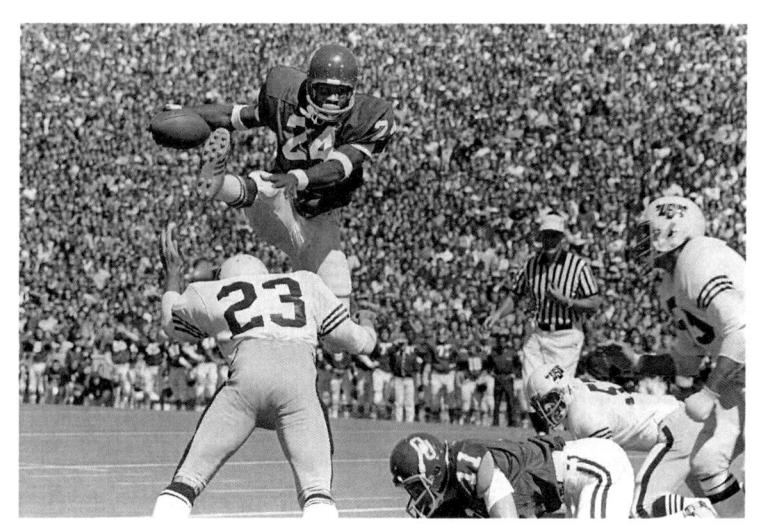

Same photo, but usually Tinker Owens (on ground and a four-year starter) is cropped out. Tink says he made this photo what it is because he didn't block #23.

Mad Dog Phillips recovered fumble vs. Nebraska. Dad on the sidelines removing my cape so I could reenter the game.

91 Sweep. Power football. No option—no deception. Right side of line fires out; left side was to pull and run over anything in their way. My job was to hide behind my lineman until the coast was clear.

Me, Archie Griffin (two-time Heisman Trophy winner, Ohio State), and Anthony Davis (USC) at All-American Awards event in Florida. Notice anything different about this photo?

Oops - I ran over a band member- hope to this day they were okay. This was my freshman year; we didn't have names on our jerseys that year.

With Coach for Touchdown Club's Pigskin Awards, 1974. Coach was Coach of the Year and I was named Offensive Player of the Year. Nice bow ties; clip-ons.

Walter Camp Awards Banquet, 1974.

The Selmon brothers—OU legends; Lucious, Dewey, and Lee Roy.

Senior year, early in the season and game. We had 'hung half a hundred' on someone. I was finished for the game and so were my shoes, but I didn't let them out of my sight.

Punt Return vs. Texas '75. In background are my two coaches- Dad (Big Joe) and Coach Switzer

One of very few days I didn't practice because of an injury. This picture was taken my freshman year when I had a hyperextended knee. The only other missed practice was for a slight shoulder separation during my senior year.

Vs. Kansas, 1975, landing gear deployed. Landing like a "butterfly with sore feet." I wonder who the kid is?

Vs. Kansas, 1975.

1976 preseason game, rookie year with Chargers vs. New England Patriots coached by Chuck Fairbanks. Game was played at night on Owens Field. I injured my knee that evening; out for the season.

First preseason game, rookie year, with Chargers in San Diego vs. the Philadelphia Eagles.

I know, cool glasses, right? I had two detached retina surgeries, 1977 and 1978 with the Chargers. I would wear goggles from there on out, until I retired. Well, I would wear them at least the first series of every game to please everybody.

Now with Baltimore-playing against the Houston Oilers and the great Earl Campbell, 1978.

Press photo with Washington Redskins team, 1981.

VS. LA Raiders, 1983, facing my OU buddy, Greg Pruitt

With the Redskins in 1983, against St. Louis. Believe it or not I was tackled by this guys cleat.

Man of the Year banquet in DC with Alexander Haig, Secretary of State-I told him he really was in charge of the country.

My brother Kim, Quarterback for North Texas. He saw Johnny Unitas do that with his hands.

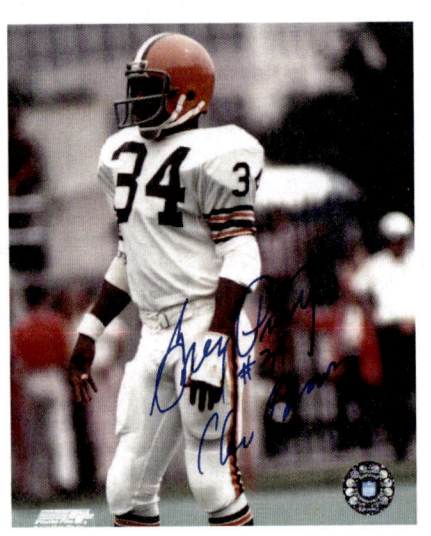

The great Greg Pruitt. One of the main reasons I attended Oklahoma.

O. J. Anderson from the University of Miami and me around 1989. O. J. was a great back for the New York Giants and St. Louis Cardinals.

The first University of Oklahoma Heisman Trophy winner - the late Billy Vessels and two "shudda, wudda, cuddas." There are a lot of guys that should have won the Heisman, but no one has won it who didn't deserve it.

*Last time I ever had those silver shoes on my feet-
Alumni Game, 1994 at OU, with Billy Sims and Greg
Pruitt. Coach Hochever is in the background.*

*Poetry in motion; all on the same foot. Billy Sims, Greg Pruitt
and me at OU Alumni Game. Billy was a freshman my senior
year at OU and I was a freshman during Greg's senior year.*

Our Hauler for Dr Pepper Car, 1998 Busch NASCAR Circuit. Our matching truck hadn't arrived yet.

Me and partner Julius Erving with Car

My favorite photo of the great Julius Erving.

Part of Race Team Crew-Texas Motor Speedway

*Me and Coach in Chicago before OU's
Game with Notre Dame 2013*

Visiting with Coach Stoops in his office at OU - a great guy and what our program needed.

Hall of Fame Awards with Roosevelt Leaks (hook 'em). We were teammates with the Colts. Another great guy.

Press conference at National College Hall of Fame, 2005. Helmet is much heavier than mine.

Saying goodbye-final game at OU. Oklahoma fans will always be number one.

SECRET #6

Just Joe

This chapter, Secret 6 is a hodgepodge of thoughts and opinions of how I view life, with some football experiences mixed in. I am a firm believer that it is good to have people you look up to and want to emulate, but we should never strive to be someone else. It is extremely important to be the best YOU God created you to be. When we reach those pearly gates, God isn't going to say, "Joe – why weren't you Billy Graham or Roger Staubach, or even my dad, Joe, Sr.?" He is going to say, "Joe, why weren't you, YOU – the only one, the original, the one I wanted YOU to be?"

The reason I have known a little success on and off the football field is because I have sincerely tried to be just me…transparent, honest, quirky at times, flawed in many ways, but I've never tried to be anyone else. So here are some random thoughts that hopefully will give you some insight into who I am as I encourage you to be who YOU are.

Am I liberal? Yes. Am I conservative? Yes. Am I moderate? Yes.

My thoughts on taxing the upper one percent economic bracket: Let's not overlook what the upper one percent does for America. For one, who do you think owns the businesses that provide millions of jobs? Do we realize how and who funds all of these philanthropic events and causes for the needy and sick around the world? It's the upper one percent! One example is Don Stevens' medical ship of volunteers that provides medical care in Africa and other places. There needs to be a way to institute tax incentives for the upper one percent in definite areas. One way would be to initiate an insurance program allowing them to donate or give to that program and receive a significant tax advantage, but we don't think about that. Remember, it's not about one side winning. Wouldn't that fund it for us?

Every now and then, I will go outside on a clear night and silently stare up at the stars in the sky. At that very moment I realize how insignificant I am in this vast universe, and how the problems that are macro in size to me, are as microscopic to the universe as I am.

There are trees on the University of Oklahoma's Jimmy Austin Golf Course that are two of the oldest trees in

Oklahoma (which says a lot considering all of the tornadoes that have passed through Oklahoma). These trees are the most magnificent trees I have ever seen! One tree appears to be perfectly balanced on both sides and has limbs that are so large that it would be the most ideal tree for the Robinson family to build their home! Its age defines its stellar strength as it has met the power of Mother Nature without ever surrendering. So out of respect for this grand tree, every time I pass by it while golfing, I nonchalantly meander over and silently place my hand on its trunk; sort of a like a "high five" approval. Anything that substantial and enduring has to bring good luck. I don't believe anyone has ever even noticed that I do this, but it has become a sacred ritual of mine.

Sometimes almighty humans forget that we are simply one component on Earth and though the other components might not move about or talk, without them we humans could not survive. Nearly every living organism plays a role in maintaining the existence of this Earth and though humans might be the ones with the most overt power (except Mother Nature) that does not mean that we should disregard what the other forces bring to the table. We must step back and view the world as a whole and appreciate the importance of every component before we make decisions that are irreversible.

Realize your insignificance.

If you have children, you will easily understand this one: somewhere between birth and about three months of age, a baby starts to show excitement and joy when he or she sees mom and dad. When this happens the baby will get the biggest grin you've ever seen on his or her face and then start kicking their legs excitedly. It is the purest joy and happiness I can think of; and it is merely because one person sees another. It is pure love. If you've ever experienced this as a parent, the recollection of the memory alone will bring you joy.

As I tried to come up with a word in my head to describe this purest sense of happiness and love, all I could think of was "butt naked happiness." It's butt naked happiness because there is nothing that this child wants other than his or her mom and dad. Nothing. Pure happiness. And when a parent sees that joy and happiness, an unstoppable force takes over and the need to hold and cuddle that child is overwhelming. This purest sense of happiness involves nothing other than a parent and a child; two humans and nothing else.

We all know that changes as a child grows, but at what point does that change occur? Is it the first time mom and dad show up with a gift and the child's happiness is then diverted from mom and dad to a gift? And once that diversion happens, does a child's mind now divide its happiness between "mom and dad" and material objects? Thus, when only "mom and dad" appear, the level of excitement isn't heightened to what it once was? Surely, it is still heightened at the sight of mom and dad, but there are other things in the universe now. Is this the beginning where we, as people, start to measure obtaining of joy and happiness by the material objects we possess?

And that's when it hit me: this wasn't our Creator's intent. All parents have witnessed the natural progression of a newborn baby from birth, basically an emotionally undeveloped existence, to the first time that baby smiles. Parents know that smile is an innate response to love, and love only. That joy and happiness is a baby saying "I love you and it is because of you that I know how to express love." It is total "butt naked happiness" because there is nothing other than love that causes a baby to express this degree of happiness. At that point, material objects are irrelevant.

That is when the Biblical story of Adam and Eve came to mind and I realized that our Creator tried to show us that we needed nothing more for happiness than each other. And though I know we will never know what would have been, had the choices not been made that day by old Adam and Eve in the Garden, I do know that the purest sense of happiness doesn't come from our worldly possessions, as proven by an infant. So make your choices wisely.

Understand that chasing worldly possessions will create a vicious cycle. You will find yourself working to purchase things you may want, but don't really need, only to support a desired lifestyle. So, here's hoping you truly love your career. Every minute you spend at work is 60 seconds out of your life; 60 seconds of living a fulfilled or unfulfilled life. Life's clock and work's clock tick in tandem with one another. In other words, choose a career with which you don't resent sharing your life's clock; the seconds, minutes, hours, months and years, and try to see and understand true happiness as it was intended, before life has passed you by and it is too late. While you are busy pursuing money are you living life or is life on hold while you are too busy pursuing money to live it?

Make sure you realize that your DNA will be passed down for generations in your family, not the building in which you work, the handbag that you carry or the car you drive. Realize what is most important. If you were only one of two people on this Earth, would the label on the handbag you carry really matter? In other words, are you really only carrying that particular brand because of what it says to others? Be careful stepping onto that roller coaster. Find the balance between working enough to meet your needs or the needs of your family as opposed to work consuming so much of your life that you don't really live it. Butt naked happiness.

I agree with the adage that "money doesn't buy you happiness." But what it does is buy choices, which in turn helps maintain serenity. Allow me to explain:

Let's take two families: Family A and Family B. Both families are comprised of a husband, a wife and three children. The children in Family A are equal to the children in Family B in terms of intelligence, looks, athleticism and gender. However, Family A has inherited wealth; Family B has not. So, let's look at how the news that the family car is in need of substantial costly repairs affects each family:

Family A gets the news. No big deal. Family A has a couple of other cars to use and the expense will not change their lives one way or another. No impact or upset as a result of this news; in fact, no one in the family gives it a second thought and life continues without so much as a bump. The demeanor of the parents in Family A is unruffled and they are emotionally unaffected by the news. The community would describe them as easy going parents with "class" because the normal day-to-day problems don't seem to rile them. The minds of the children in Family A continue to be focused on school work, extra curricular activities, normal routines, not on the needed car repairs. Anxiety in their lives is minimal and they are secure, content individuals that can devote 100% of their attention on their schoolwork, friends and personal goals.

Family B gets the same news, however, the car needing repairs is the only car they have, and they are already barely getting by financially. How will the parents each get to work and take the kids where they need to go, which is always in three different directions? The plan was to have purchased a new car by now, but the heat pump in their house needed to be replaced earlier in the year which emptied out their savings. The husband in Family B now has the pressure of having to choose between two absolute necessities: providing food for his family or fixing the car that gets him to work to earn the money to provide the food for his family. So husband and father of Family B must make the choice between fixing the car, a tangible object but an essential one, and hurting the family that he loves more than his own life. His mind races through their expenses to see what cuts can be made and the pressure mounts. Over the next several months, they adjust to a very tight budget.

Meanwhile, the kids of Family B find out about an upcoming field trip and they are so excited! They run home and tell mom and dad the news, but mom and dad don't share their enthusiasm. In fact, the news of the school trip has sparked an argument between dad and mom because of the associated cost. As the children in Family B watch the argument over their field trip unfold, a sense of sadness washes over them and the excitement over the trip has been replaced with a gray cloud. And as badly as they want to go, they now feel responsible for making their parents argue and the turmoil in the family. This emotional upset has now infiltrated into the minds of the children in Family B and has become the focus instead of the normal carefree thoughts and activities that once filled the development of their young minds. In the future, they will associate causing a problem at home when a field trip is announced and will no longer share the joy and excitement their classmates have about the upcoming trip.

Now compare the development of the children in Family A against the development of the children in Family B. The path of development for Family A's children is unscathed and steady; the path of Family B's children has bifurcated and their minds have to focus on not only the usual schoolwork, relationships, and other activities of most kids, but also on worrying about mom and dad and on how their own basic needs will be met. They learn it is difficult to share in the excitement of anything that will cost money, because they are going to feel guilty asking mom and dad when money is so tight.

So my point here is to encourage understanding of others and the circumstances that make them who they are. Maybe "Johnnie Smith's dad" really isn't a mean man, but a man who questions himself and his worth as a man when he is unable to properly provide for the innocent children that he loves so much and who are reliant upon him. The unfortunate thing is this: this could truly be a wonderful life lesson taught to the children of Family B if it had not had such a snowball impact on Family B's life. If it had been just a small bump in the road and something from which they quickly recovered, the parents in Family B could explain the importance of family financial planning and consequent cause and effect upon their children. But they'd already been down that road a few years ago and they hadn't recovered from the financial strain of prior problems, so this time the parents lost any positive attitude they could have mustered and surrendered to the unfairness of life. This time, the emotional chaos of the problem clouded so much of the husband's thoughts, in particular that the families' happier times were mere memories. The future was a bleak one.

So, I do agree with the adage that money does not "buy" happiness, but what it does buy is choices and options. Basic necessities should be available for all. Meeting a family's basic needs should not be an unattainable luxury.

You know how good you feel when you have given something to someone who is in need? It is proven that giving releases endorphins which in turn leave you feeling joyful. Philanthropy doesn't have to be in the form of money; it can be in the form of something as simple as stopping to help someone you know is in need of help. The definition of *philanthropy* is: *an act or gift done or made for humanitarian purposes.* We usually relate the word philanthropy with money; however, for the generous act to be fulfilled, there is still the need for human effort of volunteers. Many are financially unable to give money, but donating funds is only a part of any philanthropic endeavor. We will always need people to physically give of their time and efforts. In my opinion, philanthropy is an innate human characteristic that attempts to keep balance in a capitalistic society. So instead of having a government that dictates the division of goods and services and that owns businesses in its attempt to keep balance among all citizens, the citizens themselves reach out and help those less fortunate; not because they have to, but because they want to.

Let's take the recently passed healthcare law wherein the government has mandated that all must have some form of healthcare or they will be fined. See, it isn't that we all need "health insurance" per se; we need to have health *care*. We need doctors and prescriptions. So why should everyone's healthcare be affected when only a certain group is in need?

Why not approach it another way by encouraging people to give when and how they are able rather than making them give? Or by:

- Allowing doctors to provide healthcare services for individuals under a certain income level and rather than getting paid by those individuals, doctors are allowed to take a tax deduction in an amount equal to their usual billable rate.
- Allowing individuals to take a higher percentage of tax deduction if they don't need healthcare facilities or if they donate to a healthcare facility, more than what

they would get if they gave to a non-healthcare facility, say, like a museum.
- Allowing pharmaceutical companies a tax deduction if they provide free prescriptions to lower income individuals.
- Allow a doctor to work off their student loans by providing healthcare services free of charge to lower income individuals.

I really believe there are other ways to accomplish meeting needs in ways that have much less effect on the general population, plus it is much easier for individuals to give or help others when it's their choice to do so—not when it is mandatory and out of their control.

Also, let's face it, there are times in everyone's life when we are in a better place to give than other times. Hopefully, there will always be individuals helping others.

The important thing to remember with philanthropy is that there is a difference between helping someone who is down on his or her luck and enabling someone to the point that they are never stimulated enough to better themselves and/or their children. A good philanthropist must not be selfish and want to keep individuals reliant on his good deeds to fulfill his own bragging rights or ego. A good philanthropist should ensure that his giving is only a push or a nudge to help someone fly. Give a hand up and not a hand-out. Our giving should never enable someone, because once someone is enabled, he or she will no longer attempt to become; they will simply exist.

Ray Lewis, the now-retired consensus all-pro linebacker for the Baltimore Ravens, is a prime example of a contagious personality. Ray has to be 300 years old (okay, maybe not quite) but his passion, enthusiasm, and the physical presence he exuded on defense, even at his age, gave a literal picture to his teammates as to how it is supposed to be done. Ray's style of play demonstrated what it takes to win, and if you watched his teammates on defense play, it is easy to see Ray Lewis' influence. We should all play with passion for whatever our particular game happens to be.

Social media is something I find to be quite perplexing, and since it is something that is relatively new, I'm not sure if we, as a society, have realized the scope of problems that will stem from this new world. And while I'm fairly certain it is here to stay, perhaps some forethought into the ramifications of what we are doing will at least cause some to pause and think twice before posting another message.

First off, what has happened to good, old-fashioned etiquette? I do not think it is a good idea to use Twitter and Facebook as a personal diary. Since when is sharing publicly what is on your mind about someone a good thing? Proper etiquette instructs us to do exactly the opposite: controlling what you say about someone and how you say it avoids confrontation. Texting has its place but the place it has occupied the most is one of conveying communication where tone and feelings can easily and often be misinterpreted. We can learn communication in this day and age without sacrificing human kindness and feelings. Having good manners is so important yet somehow what people are writing on the internet lacks exactly that! People pretend not to be directing a vicious comment at anyone specifically, but the words they say are generally mean, painful and vindictive.

While at OU there were a couple of guys on the team who made practice and games memorable. I don't even know if they remember but, I do and it was a fun time for everyone. John Roush and Jerry Arnold were offensive linemen who were buddies, but they were constantly ribbing each other. They were like an old married couple in the huddle. They reminded you of Fred Flintstone and Barney Rubble. John would come to the huddle complaining because he got a stinger, or his shoulder hit, and Jerry would feign concern, "Ah, did you get your little shoulder hurt? You baby!" Or, Jerry would whine over his shoulder pain or ache, and John would act like he had one too, only worse! It was hilarious. These were big, tough players. They worked hard, protecting me and others, but they also laughed at themselves and made us laugh. I don't think it was on purpose, though.Oh, yes, these two guys, along with the other linemen who are mentioned in this book, were frickin' awesome!

Other starters that year included, center Kyle Davis, Terry Webb, and Ed Foster. They were very cool guys. Linemen are cool guys; they work the hardest, and are often taken for granted. These guys made an impression on others and they came to practice to get better. These guys know they aren't going to win every battle, but that didn't stop them from trying. They understood what it took to win and would eagerly embrace getting back to the drawing board and practice to correct any deficiencies as would the rest of my offensive line.

I tell young football players you make your impressions on coaches in practice; you are auditioning, that's where you get your chance to play in a game. Practice is where you learn to do the small things which make the larger things easier to get to and reach the goal of winning. Embracing great practice habits allows movements to become second nature in games; doing without thinking. That, my friend, is huge in acquiring the right skills required to win. You should practice at a more intense rate than the actual game. The guys I mentioned did that but had fun, too.

Abraham Lincoln wrote that he learned from everything and everyone. He said that every book, every person he met, each life event, presented him with an opportunity to learn something. We also learn from everything, and especially from the people around us, whether they be colleagues or those in authority over us. Each will demonstrate who you want to be; or who you do not want to be. Learn to gravitate toward those people whom you most want to emulate.

How about listening? Give yourself credit for having enough sense to pick up great ideas. You are smart enough to know wrong from right.

When we moved to Port Arthur from Bay City, Texas, I was in the sixth grade. It was 1965 and I was miserable. I hated the new town – everything about it; the food and especially the mosquitos. There was this one particular dish called boudain (a spicy sausage and rice dressing delicacy of southeast Texas and Louisiana). The first time I tasted boudain, I loved it, but refused to eat it because I thought it would mean I was okay with living in Port Arthur.

Port Arthur is part of Southeast Texas' Golden Triangle, along with Beaumont and Orange. Bordering on Louisiana, the region near the coast is low, flat and made up of marshes along the shores. However, away from the coast the terrain becomes even more flat with a few rolling hills and in some areas even some dense hardwood forests. It is a great part of the country but as a youngster I could think of plenty of reasons why I was not going to be happy there. I was leaving behind friends I had known all my life and a community where I was comfortable and happy. What I learned from that time of my life was that moving didn't mean leaving. I gained new friends but I was able to keep the good of my home town with me. The point is, I may have physically left Bay City, but I grew into a better person by learning to adjust to new surroundings and I love Port Arthur just as much and I eat alot of boudain!

If you are in conversation with a person and notice that person has something foreign on their face, or food in or between their teeth, please tell that person. They should or will appreciate it. Just communicating generally, in more cases than not, can solve a lot of issues. If there is a willingness on both sides to communicate and listen, there is always a chance to come to accepted terms of agreement.

Let me tell you about a man who has my deepest respect and admiration – his name is Daryl Bryant. I had a NASCAR team at one time during the late '90's. You know what they say, "If you want to make a small fortune, go into the racing business with a large fortune." Boy, did I find that to be true. I had a few partners and we got into the business with high, high hopes, but knew little about the culture of NASCAR. We did most things right. We went into this venture thinking we could find sponsors with the business plan, vision we had and certainly between the partners; Julius Erving, NBA basketball star, myself, Kathy Thompson, Fields Jackson and Asa Murray. We would eventually raise the money needed to get started, but we were on a short learning curve, knowing there were a lot of things to comprehend in a short period. We found a sponsor in Dr Pepper, but were still short of what was needed to race. However, with our story and plan I felt it was just a matter of us visiting other corporations and making a presentation to get the financing we needed.

The one thing we did do right, (and I use the word *we* loosely because I had nothing to do with it), was to hire Daryl Bryant as our crew chief. Daryl reminds me of the character that Robert Duvall played in the movie, *Days of Thunder*, but Daryl is really real. He had an outstanding and storied footprint in racing. Like a lot of the guys in racing it was something they did most of their lives. I didn't know a lot about Daryl before we hired him but it was evident that he loved challenges. I don't know why he would even take on this untested team in the first place; a team with a new car, new driver and his bosses were three black guys who knew absolutely nothing about racing, except for the fact racers made a lot of left turns. I guess I will have to call him and find out.

Every Monday morning after the races were held on Saturday, Daryl would fill out a detailed report to send to us. He would include info on our performance before, during, and after the races and also a list of equipment needed for the next race timeframe and upcoming schedule. Well, first of all, there wasn't a snow ball's chance in hell that Daryl would receive the money for the equipment needed and Daryl knew it, but it was his job to prepare us for the next race and part of that was asking for the necessities to run our team and just keep us informed. We didn't have the resources the other teams had, but that didn't keep Daryl from putting excellent race cars on the track every week. Our backup cars were close to being as good as the primary, but he put better cars on the track than anyone under the same circumstances and our primary cars were second to none.

Our main sponsor didn't know how lucky we were to have Daryl. They were in that "wanting so much, that you don't realize what you have" mode. With all the issues we had; salaries, expensive equipment needs, moving and traveling expenses, looking for sponsors, he would send the report, knowing he was going to have to make-do with what he had. He did his job to the best of his ability and that was it. Well, actually Daryl did his job and went beyond the call of duty. I never once heard him whine or get demanding when we just couldn't supply him with the money to meet all his requests. I also knew he had to work harder and longer to maintain two high quality race cars for each week; not just workable race cars for us, but competitive, top twenty cars. To do this, meant putting in longer hours, hiring younger kids and training them to become part of the upper echelon in their field. We had several members of our crew taken by the big boys because of Daryl's skill in preparing our guys.

Daryl remains a friend today, and I appreciate his positive demeanor, his hard work, and his dedication to the task we were asking him to undertake with little to no extra resources. He did his job without complaining once about the challenging circumstances and he always brought solutions and positive feedback. He was encouraging without the bullcrap and realistic. He always came to me with a discussion and expected feedback. By the time I got out of racing, I had nearly lost the whole closet—not just my shirt! I think about Daryl often and I appreciate his great attitude during a rough, but eye opening time. He has been a key influence in my life and still is today. If I had to share a foxhole with someone, Daryl Bryant would be my first choice!

I have yet to coin a fitting definition for those who refuse to complain about a situation and instead look for the positives and remedies. That attitude will benefit you in every possible circumstance and relationship. Be part of the solution, not the problem. If you have issues and complaints, come to the table with solutions. When you get to a place where you're just bitching and moaning, just remember everybody on this earth deals with something themselves; you aren't the Lone Ranger.

When we were growing up, the neighborhood guys would organize the ball games that were played in empty lots or fields. We would choose teams, work out our own rules. Of course, there were some fights, but there we were the next day playing with the same kids we had fought with the day before. We learned to find solutions that would help us enjoy the game – we worked things out. We had to or we wouldn't get to play and that was more important than anything else. Today, in organized sports, you have overly protective, pushy moms and dads making all the decisions, instead of giving the young people the opportunity to learn, grow and work out their own problems. Part of developing a good attitude is to look for solutions.

I never thought about coming back to the University of Oklahoma in my current capacity or any capacity. After retiring from football I established a marketing firm and enjoyed several years of success representing some wonderful clients. Then, later, when approached by Joe Castiglione, or Joe C as we call him, about this position with OU, I had to ask myself some pretty tough questions: Could I succeed in a place where all I had ever known is success? I had such a positive experience as a student-athlete here; could the second time around be successful? Can I still live up to the expectations others were placing on me? If I found that I was not suited for the job, could I risk disappointing Oklahoma fans, alumni, faculty and staff, myself? I had wonderful memories of this place and didn't want anything to spoil or detract from those memories.

I was finally convinced that I could be the right person for this job, when it was clear that it would keep me tied to my passion for sports and my love for the university. I can't think of anything more challenging I would rather participate in than representing the school at charitable functions, alumni events, fundraisers, and contributing overall to the on-going success of my alma-mater and building on its great traditions. Working with an Athletic Director who understands the importance of the former athlete after their eligibility is finished is another plus. Sure, there are specific challenges, but I have always loved challenges.

I loved the movie *The Natural*, starring Robert Redford, and the fact that the baseball player, Roy Hobbs was able to admit how much he loved the game. Who can forget when Glenn Close visited him in the hospital wearing that cool hat? It was mystic.

It is really too bad that we, for the most part, don't realize that we are capable of limiting our mistakes until we have committed them.

Speaking of taking life's opportunities, as a kid I was kind of aware of my gift to run with the football the way I did, but my hero, Billy Cannon, the 1959 Heisman winner from

LSU, was a big bruiser. I thought I would also grow into a big bruising fullback because I had huge hands and feet. My final dimensions were as yet, unknown. (Sort of like the direction I get to go in this chapter–it is unknown, too–lots of different thoughts in different directions). Anyway, every time my number was called to carry the football two things existed: one, I knew the general direction I was supposed to go and, two, it was totally unknown how I would get there. For plays we ran on a regular basis, I knew the possibilities and the capabilities. Actually for me, I was born with the God-given talent to make the possibilities of the play and my capabilities one and the same.

At this stage in my life I have paid a little more attention to the way I once ran with the football. It's almost as much fun for me to watch it now, as it was to do it.

It amazes me how much opinions differ on subjects; 500 people, 500 different views. We are a society prone to seeking heroes, and for the most part there's nothing wrong with that, but many of those we choose to look up to disappoint us. Remember, just because a person is great at something doesn't mean he is a great person. It means that particular person was given a certain skill or talent or something. Just because this guy is a great athlete doesn't mean he is an outstanding citizen. We can appreciate the skill because we can see it being exhibited, but hold on to any other opinion because you really don't know what this person is like beyond that particular skill. What that person does in most cases is to commit to working hard and giving a lot of time to that God-given skill. What you hope is that the person also works at being a decent human being, worthy of your respect in every area. Coach Switzer said many times, "Be a good citizen."

Our culture seems to build people up so that we can tear them down; make them heroes or saints when, for the most part, they have only done something extra, or a little better than most. The only difference in them and any other soul, is that they found their God-given skill, honed it, used it and then were thrust into the limelight. We never seem to realize that our heroes are only human; with the same faults we have.

Speaking of heroes, the men and women serving our nation in the armed forces should be heroes to us all. Our military people after serving 20 years only receive 50% of their pay after serving their country, yet I am told politicians serving only one year receive 100%. We really need to take care of our military people.

Something else I don't quite get. Recently, the government announced that we have done away with NASA's space exploration program, the basis for our greatest technological advancements. By merely shooting for the moon we were able to accomplish so much. And cuts to our nation's defense have been approved. A diminished military force; are you kidding me? With our technology and superior military personnel we should be feared and respected because we "carry a big stick" and will use it fairly.

And, while we are talking about heroes, my hat is off to all the kids working their way through college. Since I am back working at the university I have met, been humored by, and yes, been inspired by some pretty cool kids and I appreciate it.

Another pet peeve of mine – dings/scratches/dents on my car door from careless people parking beside my car. When we as a whole don't ding any car door, only then can we be called civilized.

True friendship will stand the test of time but you still have to work at it. Call a friend or a family member you haven't contacted for a while. Perhaps you lost contact completely. Be first to call. I will say this, I can't stand that prima donna type who has to be called first and won't take the initiative to make a call.

When I was drafted by the Chargers I met this great Charger fan who also happened to be a Sooner fan from Oklahoma, but was living in San Diego. He became a dear friend. He had a car painted in the Charger blue and gold colors with a lightning bolt along the side. When I was traded to the Colts, we kept in contact. He'd call me, and I mean bunches of times, but I didn't really call him as much, so I felt bad about that. So one night my wife said, "Joe, when is the last time you have talked to Huff?"

"Oh, it's been a year, or so," I answered, sincerely thinking that was about right.

She suggested I call him and catch up, so, I did. His wife answered and after visiting for a while she told me Huff had passed away three years before. There! Lesson learned! Stay in touch with those who mean something to you.

We all have deficiencies. We can't be great at everything but we can work on lessening our deficiencies.

I had an unbelievable love for music at a very early age. I was born in 1953 and a couple of songs I grew to love during my early years were Tennessee Ernie Ford's *Sixteen Tons* and the theme to the television show *Davy Crockett, King of the Wild Frontier*. Those songs were among my first vivid memories of enjoying songs and music. Heck, I even got the whole Davy Crockett outfit which included the raccoon hat, bowie knife and the Davy Crockett canteen! I was set to go into the wilderness and take over the wild frontier.

I found unbelievable solace in music. In most cases it wasn't so much the lyrics but the music, the beat itself and the skills of the musician playing the instrument. Thanks to my friend Kerry Jackson, I continued to enjoy all kinds of music. My favorite music had distinctive instrumental parts that I paid strict attention to – I love a good bass beat–go, Bootsy! I realized the amount of time musicians put into excel at their craft was equal to, or more than the time I dedicated to enhance my skills, so I knew it was a lot! Music was my retreat, my hiding place, my imaginary friend, my mood fixer. I did listen to the words too, and the words of this song by Carol King especially resonated with me:

You've Got a Friend

When you're down and troubled; And you need some loving care
And nothin', nothin' is goin' right. Close your eyes and think of me
And soon I will be there; To brighten up even your darkest night

(Chorus)
You just call out my name, And you know wherever I am
I'll come runnin' to see you again. Winter, spring, summer or fall
All you have to do is call, And I'll be there –You've got a friend
If the sky above you; Grows dark and full of clouds
And that old north wind begins to blow
Keep your head together, and call my name out loud
Soon you'll hear me knockin' at your door

(Chorus)
You just call out my name, And you know wherever I am
I'll come runnin', runnin, yeah, yeah, to see you again
Winter, spring, summer or fall, All you have to do is call
And I'll be there, yes, I will.
(Interlude) Now ain't it good to know that you've got a friend
When people can be so cold, They'll hurt you, yes, and desert you
And take your soul if you let them–Oh, but don't you let them.

(Chorus)
You just call out my name, And you know wherever I am
I'll come runnin, runnin', yeah, yeah, yeah- to see you again
Winter, spring, summer or fall, All you have to do is call
And I'll be there, yes I will, You've got a friend…you've got a friend.
Ain't it good to know, ain't it good to know, you've got a friend
Oh yeah now, you've got a friend.

Speaking of friends. I am of the belief that if you are genuinely good to people, people will be good to you. There are exceptions though. No matter how well you treat some people they are greedy, hiney holes. They know who they are.

While playing football at Oklahoma I learned that the guys who played the right halfback position in the wishbone had to be unselfish, tough, patient, hard workers, dependable, have a deep sense of pride, loyal to the position and be willing to sacrifice the opportunity to carry the football in order to block. They threw their bodies in amongst the chaos of violence and brutality to provide a pathway for others to make first downs and touchdowns without ever uttering a single word of discontent. These guys are among my friends whom I talk to and break bread with to this day. There's Grant Burgett, "the Toast of Stroud, Oklahoma," a great athlete, strong and fast, with a heart as big as an elephant. Also, Tim Welch, who was tough and quick. He was moved to right half from fullback during my sophomore year when Grant suffered a knee injury. The number of times Tim carried the ball dropped like the stock market, but he never missed a beat. Grant was able to return my junior year. Then there was Elvis Peacock, "the pride of Miami, Florida. "Everybody" university wanted him, one of the three fastest players on the team. Grant, during his senior year, groomed Elvis, to take over the reins of the wishbone. Actually, Grant groomed us all.

I have mentioned previously another friend, Glenn Comeaux, who was from the same high school. We came to OU together and he was my teammate and roommate until he got married after my sophomore year. For the next two years

Anthony Bryant, whom we called, "Tank", was another high school teammate who became my roommate at OU. Tank is a lifelong friend. I haven't mentioned him a lot, but he's as good as they get! Have some great memories of all these guys.

🏈🏈🏈

The first time I took a handoff in a real game (a scrimmage) was my freshmen year at my dad's high school. The play was called "26", and I loved that play, It is designed to go off tackle. Your center, right guard, and tackle block down to their left and the left guard pulls and kicks out the first guy that shows up or he tries to pin him in. As the running back, I am supposed to (might I clarify, *suppose to*) run inside the guards kick-out block or bounce outside of his pin inside block. Well, my thought was that if everyone on the opposing team was getting ready to react to what they thought I was "supposed to do," I was going to be way ahead of them.

What I liked to do was press my path at full speed to the outside as if I was going outside where I would actually go if the guard pinned his man inside. However, I also wanted the opposition to think that I was going so fast that I couldn't possibly cut inside, and, in other words, show my skills.

Now, what I could also do was plant my right foot at full speed to cut inside the guard's block and in a split second plant the left foot to come out of the pathway inside the guard, to go outside, but then again plant the right foot again to go back into the hole. Confused? Illustrations available upon request. Just go outside and try it. See, I have turned that one

| 163

"supposed to" play into a quick dive between the center and guard gap.

What you have just read through is included in the course offered before "Advanced Running Back 601". The toughest move to complete though, was planting that right foot and squaring my shoulders to the line of scrimmage and going back into the direction where I started.

I guess the whole point of telling that is that there are somethings you have got to create for yourself; put a stamp on something that is totally you. I had people along the way who nurtured my desire to do things my way.

My dad, until the day I retired from football, always gave his coaching points to me before every game whether he was there or by phone and those words were, "Run Quick." My mom, on the other hand would always tell me, "June, (again the nickname she gave me for Junior) just don't jump."

There is the right way, the wrong way, and the best way. And when there is no best way, it is because we don't want to deal with the effort involved with making the best way possible.

I took great pride in knowing that even if my feet were off the ground, I was still in control.

What comes to mind when I think of a lot of my games is being in the huddle and watching the faces of my linemen when the play called for was my time to carry the ball. Sometimes I could tell they were excited. Even when it was late in the game and everybody was tired they would spring out of the huddle and strut to the line with arrogance. Occasionally I would make eye contact and could see the confidence in me on their faces. Wow, that was a great feeling!

Many people have viewed my most famous runs on the internet. There is something I've always wanted to say about my signature moves:

"Do not try these moves at home or without adult supervision. I am an expert and the moves you have seen are beyond the basic, 'Running With the Football 101'. These moves are for trained professionals, only." Ha!

For years and years, and in some cases today, there was the struggle for equality to make sure there were no differences between races; everybody has equal rights and it *is* the law. Now, what's potentially wrong with this picture is that we are teaching our kids about the history of equality. Hang with me here for a moment. I just wonder, does teaching this history actually perpetuate the problem? For example, a little black girl doesn't really know much about this history, but her best friend is a little white girl and they are inseparable What happens when there is a Little Miss Black America Pageant and the little white girl finds out she can't participate?

A person has to, expend a lot of energy to be a grinch when he is in a very pleasant atmosphere. It's really tough to be grumpy when a person smiles at you everyday with a sincere, "Good Morning."

Not long ago, I was catching an early five a.m. flight and had only gotten to bed at three, so I was dragging and really wasn't too keen about engaging anyone with any small talk.

When, lo and behold, a family goes by with two young boys pulling their suitcases, one was around six years old and the other maybe, two. As the little one went by me, he looked up straight into my eyes and with the biggest grin he said, "Good morning!" Again, you have to work real, real hard to be a creep in that situation.

I hate asparagus, squash, zucchini, broccoli, eggplant, cauliflower, and brussels sprouts. I do eat all of them, though. It's a habit. Mom made us eat all of our food before we left the table. So, I would eat what I didn't like first and save the good stuff til last. To this day, if vegetables are placed on my plate I will eat them. But, I never go back for seconds. Funny how habits like that stay with you.

I love the game of football. People have said for years that football is a character builder. What I discovered is that the game demonstrated what kind of character you are and what kind of character you had. There are very few arenas where you can experience the thrill of victory and the agony of not performing at your best from moment to moment; must be where the phrase, "the thrill of victory and the agony of defeat," came from. Where else would a player experience such an emotional outlet, the intellectual challenge, the striving to endure, the power, the strength from physical contact? What a game! You get to hit people and it's legal. Plus, it is a hell of a lot of fun!

No one likes to be told what to do, especially those who are in charge of telling people what to do.

SECRET #7

Imagination Dreams and Creating Your Own Destiny

It was the first game of the season and younger brother Kim's first Varsity game as the starting quarterback. We were preparing to play Booker T. Washington of Houston and were standing in the south end zone of the stadium. Before we could even see the opposing team's bus, we could hear them in the distance chanting, "Who are we going to get? Joe Washington!"

Kim smiled at me and said, "Looks like they are going to get a whole lot of you tonight, Joe."

I had imagined this day for years. We had rehearsed the action countless times as kids. I would re-enact what I thought the announcer would say:

"Washington receives the play from Coach Washington on the sidelines, Washington steps into the huddle, calls the play and brings the team to the line of scrimmage. Washington takes the

| 169

snap from the center, turns and hands the ball to Washington. Washington goes right, cuts up field, puts a move on the safety, TOUCHDOWN Washington!"

With the numbers 19 and 24 on our backs we were playing in our first real game together. Well, on the first play of the game, Kim takes the ball from the center, turns to hand the ball off to me but missed the handoff and we fumbled the ball. (99.9% of the time it is the quarterback's fault if the handoff goes awry). After Kim recovered the fumble we looked at each other and laughed; not quite how I had imagined the game to begin.

I believe Secret #7 is the most important secret of all. The ability to use your imagination to create goals and then see them come to fruition is one of the true blessings of life.

—Joe

I used my imagination every day growing up in Texas. I played outside nearly year around and my mother used to say, "If you hear a ball bouncing, you know where June is. (Again, that would be me, June – mom's pet name for me instead of Junior).

We played constantly, whether it was football, basketball, baseball, cops-and-robbers, or swimming. Back then, television consisted mainly of news programs; video games had not even been thought of yet, so watching TV was of no interest to me. Except for Saturday morning cartoons and sporting events, all I wanted to do was just play. And everything we played was fast paced.

All of the boys in the neighborhood would gather to play a game of touch football, and this was where I would let my imagination run freely. I would put into action every possible gyration I had ever witnessed, from a cheetah chasing its prey, to emulating Kiki Cutter, the champion American skier racing through the gates at the Olympics.

Even indoors, I would still practice my moves by running through the house pretending that the couch was a linebacker I'd have to jump over. So, I would hurdle the couch then slide through the doorways, pretending I was every running back rolled into one while Kim pretended he was, the one: Johnny Unitas. When I had to go to bed, which I resisted as long as I possibly could, I would lie in bed and imagine myself running in slow motion, imagining every detail of every step, turn, twist, spin, fake, cut and slash, turning my back to a would be tackler and hurdling when no other escape was available. I would lie awake wishing tomorrow would hurry and come.

Everything I had envisioned myself doing was transferred unconsciously to my movements on the field the next day. See, the good thing about playing with a group of kids was that there weren't any adults around supervising and interjecting their thoughts about what we SHOULD be doing–it was all of us trying out our moves without feeling embarrassed or worried about being the subject of criticism from an adult.

Everyone has the ability to form a mental image of something that is bigger and better than what they currently are, often seeing it with the clarity of a high definition monitor. It may come easier for some, but we all can imagine ourselves being good at something.

As kids, we would make up our own plays and we figured out what worked and what didn't. It was our way of getting better, extending limits. I can honestly say that had a parent been present and overseeing how we played, some of our guys would have been too self-conscious to have ever tried some of their stuff. Adults would have been interjecting their thoughts, telling us that "wasn't a good idea," "you might get hurt," and that type of thing. We may have pushed the limits, but we were cognizant of our limits, too. This was our testing ground. It didn't matter if your move didn't work because we were all trying new moves so no one was going to give you a hard time.

We even made up games. One in particular was called, "Running Through," where one player had to try to run through a line of 15 guys without being tackled; boy, did that increase my quickness and elusiveness!

So why is imagination so critical to success, you might ask? Circumstances in today's world have stolen the rights of children to play any place, any time and in an unsupervised setting, allowing them to actually free up their minds. There are very few communities where kids can run without restricted freedom, play for countless hours without supervision, learn about life through experimentation and draw conclusions that only result from firsthand participation. Being watched and supervised prevents ingenuity and the innate development of carefree, unbridled reactions. In this day and time, parents or adults supervise physical activities to the extreme to ensure their children's safety, which sadly is out of necessity.

We have limited our children's imagination by overly supervising their every move; even play time is monitored and coached by adults. All sporting activities, including practice times, are scheduled, have time constraints and are overseen and restricted. Each move is monitored and scrutinized, squashing the very thing that develops strong, independent children and their innate and spontaneous human characteristic to merely react, to be investigative and problem solve, and to just play. Restricted play can stifle a child's decision making process as well as his independence. Adults are guiding children's growth in the manner they think it should go, rather than allowing the child's intellectual curiosity to have free reign. That freedom to grow and mature gives the child opportunity to be most like their own heroes.

We are also limiting the sports our kids can participate in. It makes no sense to me for a 9-year-old to be a specialist in one sport or one position, but most parents don't seem to have the time to have their children in more than one sport, which I understand.

Today, the safety zone for children no longer extends past the walls of our homes, and for some children it doesn't even exist within the walls of their homes. Where we once never gave a second thought to running to a friend's house or riding bikes for hours, children now have to be cautious even in their own neighborhoods and leery of every person they encounter. Out of necessity, we are orchestrating their lives and more actively guiding all of their decisions (even at play), disallowing them the natural progression of independence we once enjoyed.

While we might all agree that the influence of television and video games have caused our children to be inactive and docile, if today's dangers didn't exist and they had the choice to either be inside playing videos or outside with their friends, which do you think they would choose?

Television and video games not only prevent physical stimulation, but they prevent mental stimulation as well, as the games do the thinking for children. Sure they have to figure out how to maneuver past the bad guys and whatnot, but that isn't allowing them to imagine freely and endlessly; it is merely stimulating their ability to react to a controlled event. Do such pastimes inhibit or limit goals children set for themselves, as opposed to developing a free, unbridled imagination?

When I was a kid, we envisioned activities of fun, created them and made them come to life. Nowadays, half of that has already been done for them and they merely are reactionary. We've all heard the saying "If you can dream it, you can live it." Well, what happens if you can't dream it?

I loved to play, and to be honest, I still love to play. Would I have become the player I became had my imagination and creativity been restricted and supervised? Absolutely not!

The reason I know this firsthand is because of my experience with the San Diego Chargers. I felt the coach in San Diego over supervised and restricted my ball carrying. I wasn't free to do my thing. Without getting into a long, babbling soliloquy, I will tell this short story of my restricted ball carrying experience in San Diego. In all honesty, I have always been known to break all the rules of running with the football.

One day, we were running a simple dive play, where the quarterback takes the ball from the center, takes a step to his left and hands the ball to me as I run in a straight line (supposedly) between the tackle and guard. No matter what, even if there is no space to run I am supposed to hit it in there anyway. Well, in my whole life as a running back (even as a young dreaming wanna-be running back) did I ever just run into the line without visualizing or trying to find another space to go. But the former Chargers coach would have none of this because when I did venture into that imaginative zone, he accused me of playing sand-lot ball. He was almost right, but that is how I played the game and it was the reason the Chargers had drafted me. Suffice it to say, I was very frustrated.

The need for an imagination does not end with our childhood, we just give it a more respected/mature term as adults: vision. What if Bill Gates' "vision" had been supervised and monitored by another individual? Would the thoughts in his entrepreneurial mind have been heard and developed, or would they have been guided to stay within the parameters of what was known? Is this what we are doing to our children?

There is no limit to one's imagination; no bounds. Our minds can conjure up anything. Well, I didn't always know I was doing it, but I suppose a big part of my life was spent visualizing, too; imagining what I wanted my world to consist of. I saw my future clearly, even as a small boy. I never wished my life away, but I would dream of things I wanted to do. I never set them in the form of goals, just, "I wanna do that" or "I wanna do this." "What would it be like to do this or do that." I think at times I was envious of everything that existed in this world. I wanted to see and do it all!

Although I played several sports in high school, I really loved football. But my little brother and I always imagined our playing every sport on the planet and being awesome at them all. We imagined ourselves participating in the Olympics in track and field, swimming, table tennis, and diving, playing professional basketball, baseball – all of it and we thought it was the norm. We dreamt about playing to the best of our ability; and, oh yeah, we also all wanted to be Green Berets. These guys are the real deal, along with all units of the military, male and female.

The idea of playing football for a great university didn't present itself until the end of my junior year of high school. Up until that point I was a huge Texas fan and I still hadn't imagined going to the pros yet, because this next phase would subsequently require me to prove (again!) that I wasn't too small to play. I thought I would finish college, get married, be a schoolteacher and maybe coach a little on the side. Well, that's how I had pictured life after college. Then, the possibility of playing pro ball came along after my junior year, and with it that ever present challenge that kept punching me in the nose – the misconception that I was too small to play NFL football. There's a whole world I could have been a part of, but I was focused on meeting and disproving that challenge, rather than mapping out what my life would be.

I don't recall ever verbalizing this philosophy on reaching personal goals and I'm sure some of my peers thought I was a little eccentric, wired differently, and into myself at times. I am convinced that to be able to focus on achieving big things you have got to be extremely self-absorbed, but only within that sacred, be "the best you can be" cave, and just hope you aren't too much of an asshole in the eyes of your buddies. But, I was always driven to do those things that I had already imagined myself doing.

I recall when five games into it, the dream season that Kim and I had always talked about and imagined in high school took a not-so-funny bounce. Our dad was involved in an automobile accident, broke his hip and was lost for the season, but Kim and I were still determined and focused because we knew a district championship was still within our grasp. We were closing in on our mission to win the District and State Championships. Then, two games later in the second quarter Kim broke a bone in his left wrist which kept him out of the second half of the game. During the rest of the game I thought a lot about whether he was okay. I knew he'd need to get the injury looked at and diagnosed, but for us to win the next two games and keep this mission alive, we needed him. Kim was a tough S.O.B. and if he had full use of his right hand and arm he would be okay. So, Kim gets cleared to play the following week, even though he has a fracture in his left wrist.

Things are back on track; Kim as the quarterback, me as the running back, #19 and #24. We're ahead late in the fourth quarter 14-0 and driving for another touchdown against our cross town rivals who are also ranked in the top ten in the state of Texas. We are on their 12 yard line when Kim calls the play 28 sweep in the huddle. He takes the snap from the center, turns and hands the ball to me and at about the 6 yard line, I jump over a defender to score but my leg gets caught in the crook of his arm and elbow, as I fall into the end zone. With my momentum carrying him along, too, he lands on top of my leg. I knew immediately that my leg was broken.

That would be the last time Kim handed off the ball to me. What I remember most about that night was how I got off the field. There was no stretcher, no trainers carried me, no players shoulders for me to put my arms around. While I was laying there in excruciating pain, even before the doctor and trainer could examine me, our defensive line coach, Dick Williams, scooped me up in his arms as if he were carrying one of his kids to their bedroom after they had fallen asleep watching television. He just picked me up, walked off the field and placed me on the ambulance gurney. The injury ended my high school career, but I'll always remember Coach Williams quick and caring actions afterward. Not at all how we had imagined that season to be. Sometimes life sends you in different directions and we have to adjust without compromising our finest hopes and dreams.

The Seven Secrets of the Silver Shoes is about the development of a project, and that project is you. If you were building a robot, what personality traits would you want your (clone) to have? Let's approach building you the same way. You must visualize your own success. Pick the qualities you desire to emulate, respect those around you who warrant respect and heed their advice; yet maintain the personal boundaries that make you an individual. Get excited about this project! What could possibly be more important? Create your uniqueness. The only limitations that impede this project are those you yourself allow.

In an earlier chapter I talked about my favorite athletes and how I took something from each one. There was no one guy. I admired several players' skills in my head day and night, but I also understood that some of their great skills didn't fit me. However, I saw how someone's unique personal skills and characteristics worked for them and I wanted that for myself.

During my career I struggled with trying to adapt some skills to fit what I had imagined myself to look and perform like, but I knew deep in my heart it just wasn't me. Yet, at times I still tried to force the issue. I studied the most incredible asset from each world class athlete and tried to incorporate those assets into what I envisioned I was truly capable of doing.

"Pistol" Pete Maravich, a great basketball player with a Beatle-type haircut who wore floppy socks (by the way the socks I thought he wore were Wigwam brand so I wore Wigwam socks all through my high school and college career) had a tremendous will to work hard and the imagination to try or do almost anything. I read articles about him and made note of the similarities between us. I couldn't help but relate when I learned he was a coach's son who played for his dad's team. I read that while he was riding in the front seat of a car with his dad driving, Pistol Pete would practice dribbling a basketball outside the window while the car was moving. I also read about this move where he'd dribble the basketball and when the ball would reach the highest point of the dribble, he would draw a circle with his hand around the ball then make a no-look pass to a teammate. My version of this move was done in a football game in high school while actually carrying the football.

What really brought my imagination to fruition, though, was a determination to be honest with myself. My dad would always say you can fool everybody but yourself. Initially, I found myself in constant conflict with my alter ego. I didn't know what it was trying to tell me, but my imagination was getting way off track and running away (great song by the Temptations, by the way). There was this running form of one of my idols that didn't fit what I wanted to incorporate that kept drifting in and out of my running psyche most of my football life. Not until my final four years in the NFL and after my ACLs' in both knees were gone, was I able to keep my alter ego in check, enough so, that it wouldn't betray me. Even though my imagination was vast and tough to keep in check, without it and honesty I would have had the tendency to be just normal, and I never imagined myself being normal.

Everyone imagines something when they are young. Just ask a kid what he wants to be when he grows up. They are quick to tell you what their visions are. It's easy to dream when you are young because life hasn't filled you with negative experiences. Kids are not discouraged by past failures; they haven't had that many yet. Kids are not bothered much by other people's expectations – not yet. They are excited about life and free to dream. No kid should exist without having a dream. For a kid to not have one is a travesty and we as a society have failed that kid and shame on us.

As an adult, one reason why your imagination is so important is because it provides that visual path to the past and future. William Faulkner said, "So as adults we can't stop dreaming because it is the key to our existence." The happiest people I know are those who are always working on a dream or just thinking of taking something to another level. It can sometimes be frustrating, but I believe this is one of the most important *Seven Secrets of the Silver Shoes*. Your imagination gathers the components that are necessary to completing that unique person you are now and what you will be in the future.

Can we adults recapture the ability to dream big? Can we still have the heart of a child when it comes to envisioning what we want in life? Yes. People do it all the time. They think about where they want to be in five years, ten years. We dream about what we would do if we were financially stable.

We think about how wonderful it would be if we could pursue a certain career, field of interest, sports, etc. The reality is, that it is all we do about it, and in most cases it is no one's fault.

Remember the dream or dreams you once had? They were clear to you and attainable. They were all you thought about. Little by little, life happened to you and a thousand distractions sent you off course. The dream that once burned so bright, so beautifully, now is a mere flicker in your memory. Maybe the dream has completely faded away. Reality sets in and we realize the dream may be just a little bit more difficult to attain, but that voice keeps talking to us, tapping us on our shoulder and whispering, "It's possible, it's possible."

I truly believe dreams can be reclaimed, rekindled. Or, we can choose to dream new dreams; fresh dreams. Dreams give our life purpose, direction, focus and, even if dreams never become totally fulfilled, dreaming them gives us hope.

I often wonder if my vast imagination would have existed or even come into play without my mindset. I am not really sure I was aware of its existence from the beginning, or something I have come to realize as I progress through life. I guess I was never aware of how different I was from others until I became an adult and realized that others around me didn't necessarily have the same level of determination.

I am sure this difference was one of the main contributing factors to my success as an athlete. That same quality is evident in other successful athletes, too.

I began to randomly ask questions in a quest to prove or disprove my theory. What I'm talking about is mindset. Was the mindset of a successful athlete that much different from other individuals? My mindset was so strong that not even I could reason with it. Once my mind set a goal, my body had no choice but to follow. It was like two separate entities, and the only time my body would win over my mind was when I was hurt to the point that I couldn't move. My mind would drive my body through anything; it didn't wax and wane or give in to its aches and pains. It was like having a drill sergeant. It would totally ignore most of my injuries, making my focus on the goal scream louder than the pain I was feeling; every muscle that wasn't in pain would keep driving to achieve the goal. I have come to realize that the training alone didn't set me apart. The combination of my mindset and imagination was my biggest strength.

Here's the real kicker for this chapter: You may not really find out who you are until after you discover who you aren't. Here's another kick this time with the other foot. It is better to know and understand what you don't know than what you think you know. Life and life experiences will provide you with lessons to test whether or not you are cut out for certain careers or directions. My advice is to put yourself in enough situations so you will learn what feels most productive, most comfortable. We all learn best by doing. So, put yourself out there; learn through others, again something can be learned from the most mundane. Learn through your mistakes or the mistakes of others, don't be afraid to go another direction when the road you're on is not the one for you. Get off, turn left. Do something better yet - BACK UP!

Before we go any further, I have got to clarify a few things. I know I have basically used the words dream and imagination in an interchangeable manner. One definition Webster uses for *dreams* is *"formations of involuntary ideas or images that occur while you are asleep."* The other definition that applies here is this one: *"cherished aspirations, ambitions, or ideals."* The meaning of *imagination,* however, is as follows: *"Imagination is the by-product of your mind creating images and ideas on command."*

By the way, your dreams will most likely include or have something to do with what you are already good at. They will also represent something you would like to possess or be the creator of, or something you are happy doing. It may be something that comes fairly easy for you, making for an ideal situation. If you are going to create anything, you might as well make it great.

A good salesman more than likely already knows he has a gift of communication and persuasion. His dream may be to become the top salesman in the state, so I would imagine he would try to acquire the skills he's lacking to reach that dream. Some of us need a little affirmation about what we do and how we do it. So, seek out help with formulating your own dream, then remember to pass it forward and be available for others in the future. One task we all must conquer is to find our purpose, our calling on this God's earth and that is the reason we possess dreams and imagination to help us seek and find our unique place in the world.

In an earlier chapter I told this story about my first scrimmage with the high school varsity team. I was over on the sideline horsing around when my dad called me over to ask me if I could compete with our opponents and I said, "Yes," only to be sent back to stand with the rest of the junior varsity. My father then called me back to participate with the varsity and I played like I had always imagined I could. In that chapter, I talked about how, as a youngster, I had imagined those moments, my actions, and using my running skills.

So, I took my place in the huddle and waited for the quarterback to call the play and it was just as I had heard all my life in my imagination; slow and precise. We broke the huddle and jogged to the line of scrimmage. I got in my stance, the snap count was reached, every player moved to their assignments and I took my first steps. I came out of my stance, shoulders parallel to the line of scrimmage although my legs were perpendicular to my shoulders. I took the handoff from the quarterback and with the ball in my hands took three steps, planted my right foot to cut inside the pulling guards kick-out block. The hole was there but one of my lineman's legs was in the way. Which is really no big deal. I had imagined navigating through that situation numerous times while running through the living room of our house, where a couch or a doorway blocked my path. But this was real, and it was everything I had imagined and more.

What is the thing you do best? The answer could be part of the road map to chart the way to your own personal visions and success. Because of my size and quickness, most football people felt I personally liked running with the football outside the tackles. As far as I was concerned, sweeps were just speed plays and for the most part they were simple to run and if you had some speed you could run those kinds of plays. Now, where I envisioned my running skills being showcased was between the tackles, inside, up the middle where my quickness and ability to cut and change directions were valuable assets. Knowing your limitations becomes crucial when trying to expand your skills and do more. Realizing what you lack in most cases is just as important as knowing and utilizing your greatest assets. You have to be totally aware of your base when you are in the process of trying to do more. Sometimes we try to do so many things that we don't do any of them well. You've got to firm up that base (taking care of the little things makes the big things reachable) before you go to other things. That way you will be able to concentrate on those new things without the apprehensions that come with trying them.

Before the 1976 draft, the NFL scouts scheduled visits to various universities to check out potential candidates. When they arrived to see several of us on campus at the University of Oklahoma, I knew that my size had always been an issue for some. I was smaller than most players, but it was never an issue with Coach Switzer; he never even brought it up. Still, I knew that some of the scouts would think I was small for a future NFL running back, especially one who could be an every-down player. I usually weighed around 167 pounds. I knew I couldn't conceal my size because scouts would be looking right at me. As the weigh-in time approached, I put my imagination to the ultimate test.

Instead of coming up with a way to avoid being weighed and measured, I began to think of ways I could add a little weight and some height before the weigh-in. They stripped you down to T-shirts, socks and jocks; so there was no way I could hide a tire iron on my body. I had some heel wedges I could put in my socks that would make me look taller, but didn't know what I could do to add some pounds. Then, it came to me. If I took some of those small pegs from the ankle weights I had, put a bunch of them in each hand, then cross my arms over my chest with my fist snugged tight up under my armpits, I might stand a chance to tip the scales at a little more than what the scouts expected when I hopped on.

So, in the dressing room, before the weigh-ins, I placed the wedge inserts under my feet, taped them to my heels, and put my socks on over them. Then, I took ten of those peg ankle weights and put five in each hand. Then, I waited anxiously until they called my name for weigh-ins. I heard my name, and then walked directly to the scales, arms tightly crossed over my chest, clutching the weights in my fists under each arm, scared to death they would find me out. I had to throw in a little acting job, too, becoming a character that said by my movements, "Hey, I really don't have much time for this. You guys need to hurry and get this stuff going. If you don't get to it, you won't be able to get my weight and height." Anyway, to my great relief, it worked. I weighed about 179 or 180. I recall someone saying, "Man, he's bigger than we thought." Then, I dashed out without saying a word to anyone, knowing that I couldn't stop to socialize because there was no way I could shake hands or greet anyone before I got back to the dressing room to get rid of those weights. Yes, a little underhanded perhaps, but hey, give me a few points for creativity and imagination, okay?

I knew and everyone else knew it was out of character for me to just leave the room without speaking to people, but, Gee, I was so sick and tired of always having to address my size.

I thought I had gotten away with the ruse until my Dad called wanting to know why I wasn't as cordial as usual and if anything had been said that had caused me to be so unfriendly during the weigh-in. One of the scouts present that day had known my father in Texas and called him to report, "Little Joe, didn't stay around and he wasn't very cordial with any of us. In fact, he left without talking to anyone. He didn't stay around to meet us or visit."

Dad couldn't understand what he was being told and he wanted to hear from me. "What was wrong? This was totally out of character." I explained the whole thing to him and now we laugh about it, but he was really concerned at the time.

I was drafted in 1976 by the San Diego Chargers for less money than my parents were making at the time as school teachers. I probably should have negotiated for more, but I just wanted to play. The Chargers didn't have to promise me anything, just their drafting me first told me what they expected, giving me the opportunity to play right away.

Being smaller than most, I felt like I had a lot to prove to myself and others and just wanted to get started. Since I had been making nothing, whatever pay package the Chargers offered was more than what I had. I loved the game and I loved running with the football, plain and simple. Besides, I was getting the chance to play for one of my favorite childhood teams; the ones with the lightning bolts on their helmets.

I loved the game so much it broke my heart when I was injured at the beginning of my rookie year. I wouldn't have imagined in a million years something like that happening, and especially ironic in that the injury occurred without anyone touching me.

This was one of the most difficult periods of my life. Not only did the injury threaten my career, it threw me into emotional turmoil. It sucked the heart right out of me. I began to doubt my own God-given skills. Somehow, the vision was blurred that I could play football at the highest level. Then, I made a commitment to embrace my visions anew. I worked hard and simply refused to relinquish the vision I had as a do-everything running back in the NFL. I came back from the knee surgeries, and had a fair season by my standards. Then, after two years in San Diego, I was traded to Baltimore where a new beginning awaited and a chance to prove what I knew all along. One of the things I was put on this earth to do was to carry the football in a manner all my own. Most of all, I could continue doing what I loved.

Because I had been the number one draft choice, the team's expectations were so high and at this juncture, those expectations had not been met. The thought of what could have been, had I been healthy, was disappointing and haunting, but it was time to move on.

The process for fulfilling your visions may not always be clear or easy and it isn't easy to be patient while your visions become clear. You may fail, fall down, mess up, have bumps and bruises, but dream big anyway. Life is an adventure. It's like an amusement park thrill-ride. The roller-coaster may be huge, twisting and fast. You get on, knowing it will be scary. You face your fears anyway. You get on, strap in and ride. Then, wow! This is fun! You did it and even may want to ride again! Same with your dreams. There is an immense joy in anticipating and then seeing the dream all the way through. It meets a deep human need for excitement, discovery, and fulfillment.

My conscious is and has been a driving force of checks and balances in my life and a policing element in my decision making. With that being said, the quote my dad always used comes to my mind again, "You can lie to and fool everybody, but yourself." My mom had a saying she used, too. She'd always remind or tell me and my siblings before being punished, while wielding that belt or switch, "You knew it was wrong when you did it, didn't you?"

My penchant for putting myself in someone else's place made me more aware of the feelings and motives of others. Also, on a side note, sometimes we feel it is too late to apologize but, in my opinion you should do it anyway, even if only to outwardly admit to yourself that you should apologize.

The vision of this book (well not this exact book but a different book) kept popping up in my head until I finally mentioned it to my accountant and loyal friend, Lloyd Trenary. Lloyd and I had been like father and oldest son, accountant and client, business partners and a person I would always run things by for almost forty years. So I was just casually mentioning it to him and he suggested I talk to a friend and client of his who is a publisher (the publisher of this book).

The publisher suggested the title and the type of book you are reading now which was at the opposite end of what I was thinking. I certainly wasn't thinking in these terms and I hadn't envisioned being an author, but he convinced me that it made sense. I have always enjoyed speaking and sharing stories and my personal views of sports and my life. I have spoken across the country at various sporting events, awards banquets, seminars and conferences, so when presented with this opportunity to author a book, I had to really visualize this total commitment and what the end product would be. I was finally convinced that there were some things I could share that hopefully would make a difference in the lives of others. I feel fortunate to have an opportunity to share *The Seven Secrets of the Silver Shoes* with those aspiring to be all that we were created by God to be. Sadly, my friend Lloyd passed away in July of 2012 before the book was completed and released.

Others have passed away, too—men I admired, emulated, and with whom I shared a special brotherhood. Coaches Port Robinson, Gene Hochevar, and Wendell Mosley are gone. Great teammates like Steve Davis, Rod Shoate, Dennis Buchanan, Lee Roy Selmon, and others are no longer with us.

This journey called life reminds me of nothing and of everything. In a sort of vague way, life lessons get you in the right shape or frame of mind for life. It reminds me of working out, getting in shape for a long season, knowing that there were going to be games with high productivity and then there were going to be days where your running skills were at their finest, but your yardage output was dismal. That's why you play the games, you never know exactly how they will turn out.

I cannot possibly begin to count the number of times I ran the stadium steps in Port Arthur during the hot, humid summers, rain or shine. I ran them when it was so hot I begged God for just a cloud, a tiny bit of a breeze, anything to relieve my sweltering body as I climbed the stairs, row after row, up and down, again and again, knowing there wasn't a snowball's chance in hell of that happening. As I ran, my imagination took me to the Cotton Bowl for the annual Texas vs. Oklahoma shoot-out, knowing the temperature on the turf would be in excess of 120 degrees. No substitutions and no timeouts and me pushing my almost dehydrated 170 pound frame till the end. That is what got me through. Those stadium steps were what my mindset was created for. Nothing better for conditioning than stadium steps.

There is a film somewhere, (Dad lent it out to someone), showing me running the stadium steps and it is pretty good. You see, I didn't have to look at my feet going up or down because the footwork was so quick that it would throw me off and I would fall down the stairs if I actually looked, so I used the visual lens in my mind. I would sometimes run the steps in the dark.

Like running stadium steps, success often depends on what you are willing to pay for it. My effort was rewarded when I improved my quickness, endurance and strength. Your dedication to pursue your own goals for success will be much more satisfying when you know the time, effort, and focus it took to achieve them.

My imagination has been my life saver. A place where I could visualize and analyze the whole situation when the going got tough, not only in football but in real life. My imagination was my practice game. I would often fall to the ground when I finished running those steps, exhausted, but with a deep satisfaction that I had done it – I had finished.

Finishing. What an important word. I have known runners who competed in races while constantly visualizing that finish line. Through each grueling stride and gasp for air, when their legs are about to give out, and lungs are about to burst, when every muscle is shouting, "Get that guerilla off our back!" they press on. They continue because the goal they have visualized is not complete until they cross the tape and that medal is placed around their neck. That medal says, "Done!"

Marathon runners when they finish after hours of putting strides together are so spent that many of them fall into the arms of greeters as they finish, but they are also elated. Many shout, some collapse to their knees in utter joy, others weep. They have finished! Many of these runners will never actually win by having the best time in a race, but their victory is found only in crossing the tape; finishing.

Life is like that. It's being competitive with your greatest opponent, you. It's about doing your best and always going one step further when you don't think you can. It is a commitment to just keep on doing life and working on your dreams until you reach life's finish line.

Your dream may not be completely fulfilled in your life time. It's the going for it that counts. Someone else may pick up that dream and run it in all the way for you. Like a lateral on the football field, you hand it off so someone else can run in and make the TD.

Dreams are caught just like that. We must mention the riveting declaration of Martin Luther King's "dreams" that forged change and tolerance in a racially divided country. I make mention and reproduce his words here because to have that kind of vision and commitment is very special. He passed the dreams along for further generations:

> *"I have a dream* that one day this nation will rise up and live out the true meaning of its creed: 'We hold these truths to be self-evident, that all men are created equal.'"
>
> *"I have a dream* that my four little children will one day live in a nation where they will not be judged by the color of their skin, but by the content of their character."
>
> *"I have a dream* that one day on the red hills of Georgia the sons of former slaves and the sons of former slave owners will be able to sit down together at a table of brotherhood."

King's dreams inspired millions to dream the same dreams and our nation has never been the same. These quotes are also familiar to most of us: "If you dream it, you can be it," and "If you believe it, you can achieve it!" These words aren't just "New age" mumbo-jumbo: the sayings are true. What we think about most is who we are. When we give ourselves freedom to dream and dream big, we are creating our future.

The poem below, written in 1875 by William Ernest Henley, has inspired many, among them Nelson Mandela. He quoted the poem often to fellow prisoners during his incarceration, and was personally empowered by its message of creating your own destiny. I first heard it from a friend of mine, Reggie Williams, who went to Dartmouth and played for the Cincinnati Bengals

INVICTUS

Out of the night that covers me,
Black as the pit from pole to pole,
I thank whatever gods may be
For my unconquerable soul. In the fell clutch of circumstance
I have not winced nor cried aloud.
Under the bludgeonings of chance
My head is bloody, but unbowed. Beyond this place of wrath and tears
Looms but the horror of the shade,
And yet the menace of the years
Finds and shall find me unafraid. It matters not how strait the gate,
How charged with punishments the scroll,
I am the master of my fate:
I am the captain of my soul.

May your dreams burn brightly no matter what they are and keep you focused even when it seems impossible to others. When I look at or hear of anything that pertains to my football playing days, I think of that little kid in a small town in Texas who imagined all kinds of things and none of them were ever about championship rings. Then, with the help and support of my village, I followed the path that was made for me and tried to hurdle, dodge, plant and cut and navigate that path by being a good steady cleat on a football shoe. The visions are still impacting my life today.

Because I learned these life lessons, I can hopefully help others understand them. They are the same for all. Striving for your dreams and using your imagination can be keys to finding your purpose on earth. One other thing about your dreams, they take you anywhere you want to go without physically leaving. You can do anything you dream of without lifting a finger and your imagination can give you as many trial runs as you may need.

Harriet Tubman, the runaway slave from Maryland, dreamed of freedom. After finally gaining her own freedom, she created the "underground railroad" which helped hundreds of slaves find their own freedom, too. That is what dreaming does; it inspires others to dream. Tubman, who became known as the "Moses of her people," wrote:

"Every great dream begins with a dreamer. Always remember, you have within you the strength, the patience, and the passion to reach for the stars to change the world."

And then...

Seems like it was yesterday that I was hightailing it down the street to meet my neighborhood buddies for a pick-up football game or even a game of cops and robbers.

And wasn't it just the other day I wore the crimson and cream colors of the University of Oklahoma while listening to Coach Switzer tell us to "go out there and put half a hundred on 'em?"

Had to be just recently that I held my baby daughter, Brandy, in my hand, knowing that I couldn't fumble now, or anytime while she grew into adulthood. I marveled at the awesome responsibility and privilege of parenthood. Now Brandy is a lovely, cool young woman newly married and looking forward to building a family of her own.

Again, I was privileged to live the ultimate dream of my life, playing with my brother, and for my dad. I probably could have quit after accomplishing that dream, but quitting in any shape or form was not part of our DNA. I believe we were put on this earth to help people make a difference and leave this place better than we found it. My playing professional football did give me a platform to do things and hopefully some were good. It also gave me the chance to live in and play for some great cities. I still live in the great city of Baltimore, with great memories of my playing days.

Wow, seems like that was just a day or two ago. Where does the time go? And when it is all said and done, what will really count as success? In the end, doesn't it all come down to the things that were important from the beginning?

The Seven Secrets of the Silver Shoes are really not secrets at all. These principles have been around a long time. I may have said and applied them a little differently in this book, but it still comes down to a few things: do your best always, get back up every time you get knocked down, dream big dreams. And for God's sake, treat people the way you want to be treated—be respectful, considerate and nice to people.

Now by no means do I hope this moment comes soon, but one day a memorial service will be held because Joe Washington has hurdled the last would-be tackler. Old teammates and I joke that God has yet to miss a tackle and one day He'll get us all. Anyway, I have always thought about that time and have hoped that people could say some good things about me, and hopefully more good than bad. Maybe I had a positive effect on someone's life. If I hurt anyone, I apologize. And maybe folks will know how much I loved running with the football and will say, "Oh, yeah, he was the guy who wore the silver shoes."

—Joe

SPECIAL THANKS

Thanks to JJ for your insight, out-sight and focus. Thanks for making sure this book was "Joe" and that it did get finished.

Thanks to friend and photographer extraordinaire, Bart Brag, who provided the high school photos.

I would like to give a special "thank you" to Rita Tate, who not only is an integral part of Tate Publishing, but a dear friend. Thank you for your unwavering patience and understanding throughout the writing of this book. I've lost count of the number of times I'd given you a "completed" chapter to edit, and I would take it back and change everything! While I'm pretty sure those countless changes were challenging and frustrating to everyone, you never showed it. Thank you for accepting that I had to do it my way; thank you for not becoming exhausted and giving up on me, and thank you for your continued support during this journey. You made this an enjoyable and memorable experience for me, and one that would not have come to fruition without You. Also, to Bob

West, sports editor of my hometown newspaper *The Port Arthur News*. Thanks, Bob, not only for your input, but also your friendship and unwavering support for my entire life.

—Joe

e|LIVE

listen|imagine|view|experience

AUDIO BOOK DOWNLOAD INCLUDED WITH THIS BOOK!

In your hands you hold a complete digital entertainment package. In addition to the paper version, you receive a free download of the audio version of this book. Simply use the code listed below when visiting our website. Once downloaded to your computer, you can listen to the book through your computer's speakers, burn it to an audio CD or save the file to your portable music device (such as Apple's popular iPod) and listen on the go!

How to get your free audio book digital download:

1. Visit www.tatepublishing.com and click on the e|LIVE logo on the home page.
2. Enter the following coupon code:
   afef-2887-2924-c906-7ca8-3423-f585-d938
3. Download the audio book from your e|LIVE digital locker and begin enjoying your new digital entertainment package today!